FUSING FABRIC

FUSING FABRIC

Margaret Beal

BATSFORD

ACKNOWLEDGEMENTS

I must first thank my husband Andrew for the continuous help and support that has made it possible for me to write this book.

My thanks also go to Jo, who has helped and encouraged me over many months, to Tracey and Cindy, who have tried and tested the text and many of the methods, and to Michael Wicks and Andrew Smart for the beautiful photography.

Finally, I would like to thank the many friends and embroiderers who encouraged me to write this book.

First published in the United Kingdom in 2005
First published in paperback in 2007 by
Batsford
10 Southcombe Street
London
W14 0RA

An imprint of Anova Books Company Ltd

ISBN: 9780713490688

A CIP catalogue record for this book is available from the British Library.

10 9 8 7 6 5 4 3 2 1

Reproduction by Anorax Imaging Ltd, Leeds
Printed and bound by SNP Leefung Printers Ltd, China

This book can be ordered direct from the publisher at the website: www.anovabooks.com, or try your local bookshop.

Photography by Michael Wicks unless otherwise specified.

Distributed in the United States and Canada by Sterling Publishing Co., 387 Park Avenue South, New York, NY 10016, USA

Page 1 A small panel combining mark-making, cutwork, reverse appliqué and a relief effect (photograph: Andrew Smart).

Page 2 This panel was created by bonding fragments of organza to Wireform Sparkle Mesh. The Wireform was then cut into strips, which were rolled around a pencil to form straws.

Page 3 Three-dimensional bubbly, scrunchy-textured surface created by tying pebbles into three layers of nylon organza, then steaming. The scrunchy texture was created with the soldering iron. By Pauline Miles.

Contents

Right
Book cover created using simple
mark-making techniques.

Introduction

For many years the fashion industry has used heat to bond, cut and make textured marks and patterns on fabric, and this has influenced me in the development of my own ideas for using a soldering iron on synthetic fabric. The resulting techniques and methods in this book have developed over many years by trial and error, and all are based on traditional embroidery or textile techniques.

If you have never tried heat techniques, you will be unaware just how exciting and creative they can be. Mark-making, cutting and bonding are the three basic methods used throughout the book. By combining all three, with or without stitching, magical effects can be achieved.

The methods have been planned so that each one will naturally lead on to the next. For this reason, I recommend that you work through them in the set order. If you give yourself time to experiment, you will discover the magic and realize the potential. You will find that your mind will soon be full of ideas for developing and combining ideas with many other mixed-media embroidery techniques – the 'what if ?' factor will have kicked in!

I continue to experiment with new ideas and with fabrics that I have not used before. I hope you will enjoy using this book and will discover ways of using the soldering iron that I have yet to consider.

Right
Organza shapes were bonded to PVC on acrylic felt and covered with a design traced on paper nylon. The design, which was taken from *Art Nouveau* by Edmund V. Gillon (Dover Pictorial Archive Series), was scored on the traced line with the soldering iron through all the layers, but only lightly into the felt. Using the reverse appliqué technique, most of the paper nylon was cut back to reveal the colours beneath.

Basic tools and equipment

SOLDERING IRON

You will require a soldering iron (A) with a very fine tip. Mine has a very sharp, fine tip – size 0.12mm (approximately $\frac{1}{200}$in) – and looks like a well-sharpened pencil. It uses 18 watts. Because the tip is so fine, all the heat is concentrated on the point, which means that it will cut and score very neat, sharp marks into fabrics. The temperature is also very important: if it were too hot, the fabrics might be reduced to a sticky goo; if it were too cool, you might find that some fabrics would not melt as readily as you would like. It usually takes from three to four minutes for the soldering iron to reach its full heat, but once hot it will stay hot until switched off. Soldering iron tips do wear down, but can be replaced. Angled fine-pointed tips are also available.

The soldering iron is also available with a special silicon flex, which will not melt if you accidentally touch it with the tip of the hot iron.

A

SOLDERING IRON STANDS

Manufactured soldering iron stands (not pictured) are readily available in a variety of forms. Those that clip onto the workbench are very useful. With this type, the soldering iron sits in a metal coil. A word of warning, however: the metal coil gets hot and it is possible to burn yourself on it.

I use an upturned terracotta flowerpot as a stand. This also gets a little warm, but the pot makes quite a safe place for the tip of the hot iron. Choose a pot big enough for the tip of the soldering iron to sit safely in the drainage hole, with the handle sticking up. The pot must be sufficiently tall so that the tip of the iron cannot touch your workbench, and wide enough for the tip not to touch the sides.

PROTECTIVE FACE MASK

Because of the risk of inhaling toxic fumes from melting fabric, it is advisable to wear a protective face mask or respirator (B) and to work in a well-ventilated room. An extractor fan is also useful.

GLASS

You will need to work on a piece of ordinary picture glass (C), A4 size or larger. To avoid cutting yourself, cover the edges with masking tape.

FINE WIRE WOOL

I use fine wire wool – a very soft grade 0000, pushed into a cardboard tube (D) – to keep the tip of the soldering iron clean. This prevents a build-up of melted fabric spoiling the tip and inhibiting the efficiency of the heat.

METAL RULERS

You will need a range of metal rulers in a variety of widths, but a short, thin smooth-edged ruler (E) is ideal for most of the techniques.

A safety ruler (F) will keep your fingers safely away from the tip of the iron. This type has a recess for your fingers, but unfortunately it also has graduation marks, which sometimes hinder the tip of the soldering iron from running smoothly along its edge.

Normally used to hang a picture on a wall, a mirror plate (G) makes an extremely useful small ruler. I use one all the time, because it is practical and safe, and I recommend that one of these becomes part of your basic tool kit.

B

D

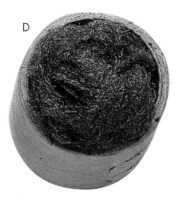

C

E

G

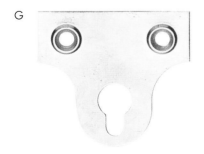

F

Other tools and equipment

Left and below
A variety of templates, both custom-made ones and 'found objects', can be used for cutting out shapes and mark-making.

METAL TEMPLATES

A variety of flat metal templates (pictured on opposite page) can be used for cutting out shapes and for mark-making. Start collecting by looking in junk boxes, tool boxes or charity shops for badges, brooches, earrings, medals, keys, grids – absolutely anything made of metal that will rest flat on the fabric.

Manufactured metal templates and stencils are very useful; a wide range of patterns and lettering is available in craft shops.

WIRE CUTTERS

These are used to cut metal grid.

HOT AIR TOOL

A hot air tool designed for craft purposes, which is hotter than a hair dryer, used to distort the surface of acrylic felt.

IRON

This is required for ironing Bondaweb (fusible webbing) to fabric.

SEWING MACHINE

A basic machine with straight and zigzag stitches, and the facility to drop or disengage the feed dogs to allow free-machine embroidery, is all that is required.

MACHINE NEEDLES

You should have a variety of machine needles, appropriate for the thread or fabric being used. These will include twin and jeans needles.

HAND SEWING NEEDLES

You may also wish to add hand stitching, in which case you will require a range of needles for hand stitching, including a medium-sized tapestry needle (also used for the reverse appliqué technique).

EMBROIDERY HOOPS

You may require hoops both for free-machine embroidery and for hand stitching. The inner hoop should be bound with tape to prevent the fabric from slipping.

Fabrics

SYNTHETIC FABRICS

These will melt with the heat of the soldering iron, so many of the methods in this book use small pieces of synthetic sheer fabric. Now is the time to use up all the bits and pieces that most embroiderers hoard and save to use someday. Look for interestingly textured synthetic fabric in charity shops or at jumble sales, bearing in mind that a dull-looking fabric can quite often be transformed when layered or mixed with a sheer fabric. The range of fabrics to look out for includes the following:

- Nylon organza (ideal for getting to grips with many of the techniques)
- Polyester
- Synthetic sheers, both plain and patterned
- Nylon chiffon scarves
- Nylon pearl organza
- Synthetic net or lace
- Foil-coated fabric
- Synthetic velvet
- PVC
- Lamé
- Glitzy fabrics

ACRYLIC FELT

Available in a wide variety of colours, acrylic felt is firm and compact. It does not have to be stretched in a frame, and its depth is ideal for mark-making.

NATURAL FABRICS

Natural fabrics will singe or burn; they will not melt. It is nevertheless useful to add some of the following types to your collection:

- Silks
- Silk organza
- Metallic fabrics
- Linen scrim
- Cotton velvet

Opposite page
Top: Acrylic felt and nylon organza.
Bottom: A selection of lightweight synthetic fabrics.

Threads

MACHINE EMBROIDERY THREADS
Test all threads with the soldering iron before using them to make sure they won't melt when they come into contact with the heat. I recommend any natural threads, such as cotton, silk and good-quality rayon machine embroidery threads. Metallic threads should also be tested before use.

THREADS FOR HAND STITCHING
You can use a wide range of silk and cotton embroidery threads to embellish your work.

Left
A selection of hand and machine embroidery threads.

Opposite page
A mixture of lightweight synthetic fabric fragments bonded to a base of polyester fabric with the soldering iron.

Other materials

When you become confident with using the soldering iron, you will want to go on to experiment with different types of material and embellishment. The following materials can be very useful:

- Wireform
- Metal grid
- Stencil film
- Foil
- Bondaweb
- Parchment paper
- Mountboard

To add further colour to your work, try collecting various painting tools and colours:

- Acrylic paints
- Metallic acrylic paints
- Water-soluble paint (I use Brusho)
- Brushes
- Sponges
- Printing blocks
- Permanent markers
- Spray paints

Below
Metal grid and Wireform.

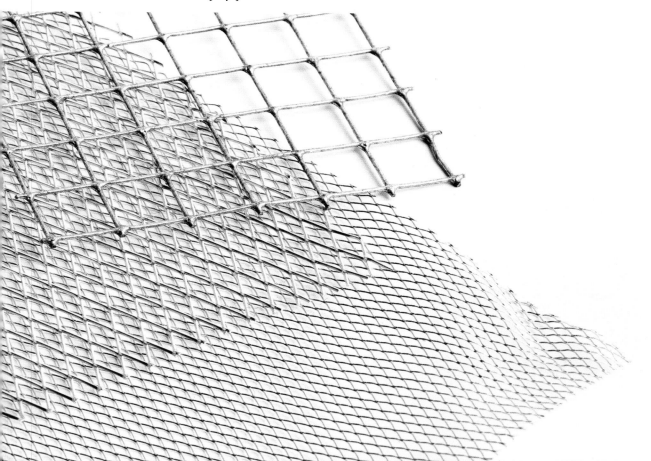

Health and safety

There are some very important dos and don'ts to observe before you start using a soldering iron.
- Do prepare a safe place in which to work.
- Do not have any extension leads or sockets on the workbench; they should be on the floor.
- Do not let leads from other equipment, such as sewing machines, lamps and extractor fans, go anywhere near the soldering iron.
- Always work on a piece of glass with masking tape around the edges.
- Always wear a mask suitable for protection from fumes.
- Always work in a well-ventilated room or use an extractor fan.
- Always remember to switch off the soldering iron when you have finished working.
- Have fun!

General hints and tips

Bear these tips in mind as you work through the techniques in the book:
- If you find that a seam has not perfectly sealed, you probably need to put more pressure on the fabric with the ruler. Tilt the ruler and press the edge firmly on the fabrics to exert more pressure on them.
- Stabilize very flimsy and loosely woven fabric by bonding it to a nylon organza.
- Bond heavyweight stretchy fabrics, such as PVC, to acrylic felt to stabilize them.
- Lightweight, flimsy fabrics tend to stretch. To avoid puckering, it will help if you use a small running-stitch mark along the edge of the ruler, instead of one continuous line.
- Bonding and sealing two or more awkward fabrics together will often be more easily achieved if you hold the tip of the soldering iron at a very upright angle against the ruler.
- Make use of less exciting fabrics by bonding multiple layers together to create a very substantial starting point for other projects.
- A respirator will make a temporary indentation on your face. I recommend that you stop working within three hours of going to a social event, because the marks do not disappear very quickly.
- Remember to keep cleaning the tip of the soldering iron with fine wire wool as you work.

CHAPTER ONE
MARK-MAKING, CUTTING AND BONDING

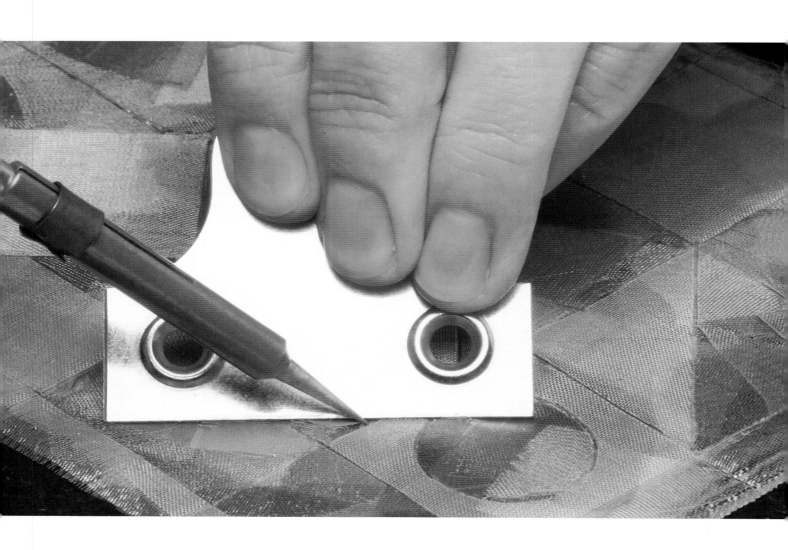

Mark-making

Making marks with the soldering iron will change the surface quality of a fabric from smooth to textured or from plain to patterned.

CHOICE OF FABRICS

For mark-making, it is important to have some depth of fabric for the tip of the soldering iron to score into. To begin with, I recommend using nylon organza on a base of acrylic felt. These are by far the easiest fabrics to use and they are available in a wide range of colours.

Acrylic felt is firm and compact, it does not have to be stretched in a frame, and the depth is ideal for mark-making. I personally use standard-size felt, measuring 23cm (9¼in) square, for most methods. Having a little extra fabric to hold onto when using the soldering iron or when stitching allows for ease of movement and control of the work. It also allows the work to grow, if you would like this. The choice of size for all methods is, of course, yours.

Nylon organza is a very thin, smooth, transparent fabric. Available in bright colours, it also has the advantage of being inexpensive. It bonds and cuts very easily with the heat of the soldering iron. Layering three or more pieces onto the acrylic felt produces an ideal surface for mark-making.

GETTING STARTED

Firstly, assemble all the basic tools and equipment (see pages 8-9). The hardest part of using the soldering iron is getting used to holding it comfortably. In fact, this is just like using a new fountain pen: it can feel a little awkward to begin with, but with practice you will soon get used to it.

Place the tip of the soldering iron safely in the drainage hole of your flower pot or in the soldering iron stand, then plug it in. It usually takes between three and four minutes to reach the maximum heat, but once hot it will stay hot until switched off.

Before making marks with the soldering iron on fabric, practise drawing lots of stitch marks on paper, as in the diagram below. Note that stitch diagrams are usually made up of short, straight and curved lines.

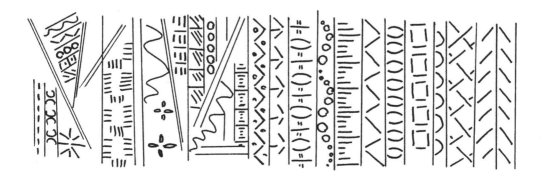

Far left
A mirror plate makes an ideal small ruler.

Simple mark-making

Inspiration for mark-making can be taken from many sources: look, for example, in stitch books on canvas work, blackwork, whitework, Hardanger, drawn-thread work, broderie anglaise and many more styles of embroidery. In addition to your basic tools and equipment, including a metal ruler and mirror plate, you will require one piece of acrylic felt in a strong colour, plus three pieces of nylon organza, in contrasting colours, the same size as the felt.

Method

1. Place the felt on the glass with the three pieces of organza layered on top.
2. Place the ruler on the fabrics, approximately 2cm (³/₄in) down from the top.
3. Run the tip of the soldering iron slowly along the edge, pressing deeply enough so that a visible line is scored into the felt, but not so deep that you cut right through to the glass. The organzas will have bonded to the felt.
4. Slide the ruler down the fabric and mark rows of lines, about 6cm (2½in) long and with gaps between them varying from 5 to 10mm (¼ to ½in) wide, as if ruling a page in a book.
5. Now refer to your stitch mark patterns and, holding the tip of the soldering iron at a fairly upright angle, slowly make marks between the lines, either freehand or along the edge of the mirror plate. The tip of the soldering iron will score into the felt and the colour of the felt will show through. Marks made along the edge of the mirror plate will be neater and sharper than marks made freehand.

Far right
Two panels made using a variety of mark-making techniques. Kindly loaned by Robin and Diana Kent.

Right
Lines and stitch marks made on nylon organza on a base of acrylic felt.

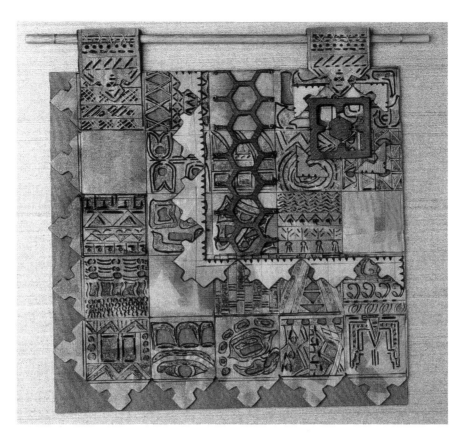

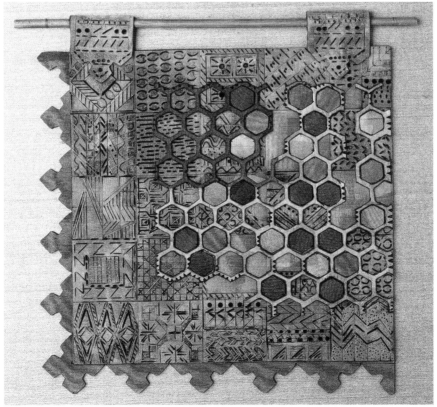

Eyelets

The tip of the soldering iron makes perfect eyelets, in circular, oval and droplet shapes.

ROUND EYELETS
1. As before, run the tip of the soldering iron along the edge of the ruler to mark a few lines.
2. You need to hold the work off the glass to make the eyelets, so be careful not to burn your fingers.
3. Gently and slowly push the tip of the soldering iron vertically through the fabrics and then slowly withdraw it vertically. The size of the eyelet will depend on how far you push the tip through the fabric.

OVAL AND DROPLET-SHAPED EYELETS
Press the tip of the soldering iron into the fabric and lower it, at a shallow angle, deep into the felt, but not through to the glass. Experiment using other fabrics and adding many more layers; the marks will be very deeply embedded in the fabrics. A possible design incorporating eyelets of all types is shown below.

Further suggestion
*   To add more interest, cover the felt with an iridescent organza or other glitzy fabric before layering the three pieces of nylon organza.

Top right:
Eyelets threaded with wool yarn.
Near right:
Sample using droplet-shaped eyelets.
Far right:
Sample using round eyelets.

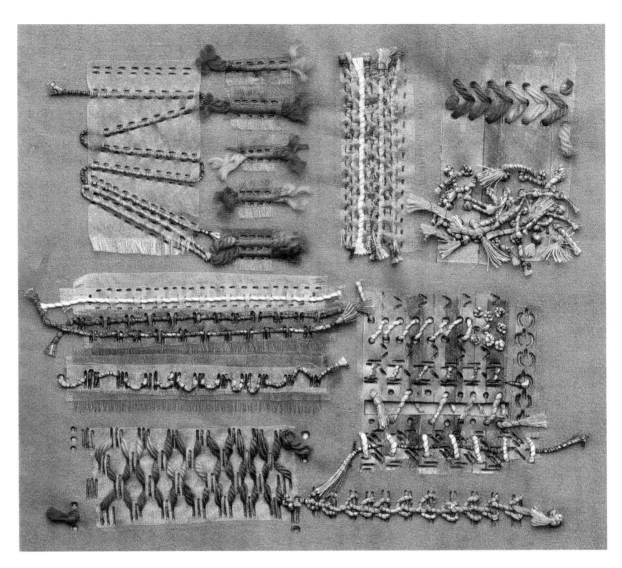

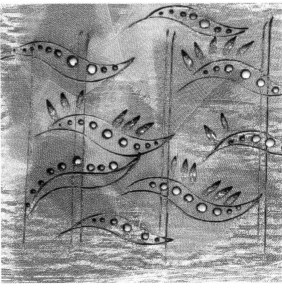

Scoring fine lines

In the previous method, a base of acrylic felt was used to give depth for the soldering iron to score into. The following methods are worked on at least five or six layers of nylon organza or other lightweight non-stretch polyester fabric, patterned or plain. The tip of the soldering iron scores into the layers, blending the colours and any frayed edges together. The more layers of fabric you use, the deeper, stronger and darker the lines or grooves will be. In addition to your basic tools and equipment (which should include a mirror plate: see page 9), you will require two pieces of nylon organza for the base, plus nylon organza in a variety of colours, cut into rectangles and squares in a range of sizes.

Method

1. Place the two base pieces of organza on the glass and cover them evenly with the cut shapes to a depth of three or four layers, overlapping the edges generously. See diagram A, opposite.
2. Hold the mirror plate tilted on the edge of an organza shape that is roughly in the middle of the work. Run the tip of the soldering iron along the edge of the mirror plate to bond the shape to the fabrics beneath. Bond a few more edges in other areas – just enough to hold the work together and make it easier to work with.
3. Moving to the top centre of the work, place the edge of the mirror plate on the edge of one of the pieces and score a line deep enough into the fabrics to mark a groove, but not so deep that you cut through to the glass.
4. Move down that block of colour until it is covered with fine grooves with very narrow gaps between them.
5. Move to another block of colour and repeat the process.
6. Continue scoring over the blocks of colour, cross-hatching lines and varying the spaces between them until the whole piece is scored and all the blocks of colour are blended together (see diagram B, opposite). Further pattern suggestions are given in diagram C, also opposite.

Further suggestion

• Machine-embroider a design over the scored lines.

A Overlap the cut shapes generously.

B Score marks are made over the blocks of colour.

C Scoring fine lines forms a pattern.

Above
Blocks of colour layered on a base of nylon organza, scored with fine lines and grooves.

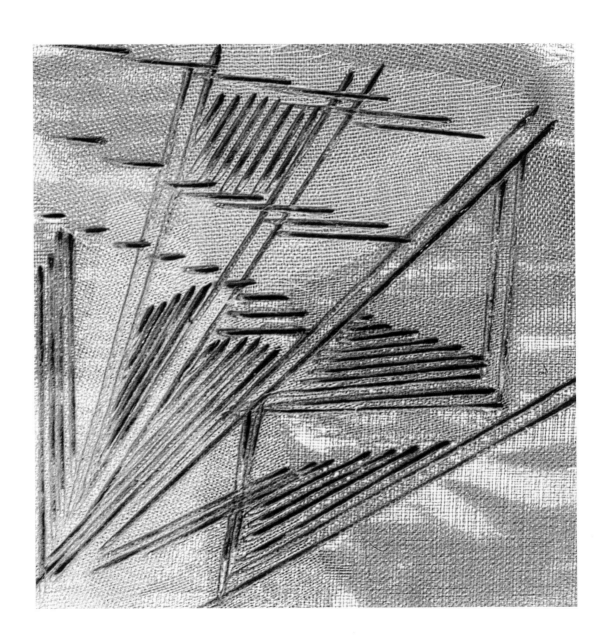

Above
Lines scored onto white foil-coated
fabric on a base of acrylic felt.

Mark-making, cutting and bonding

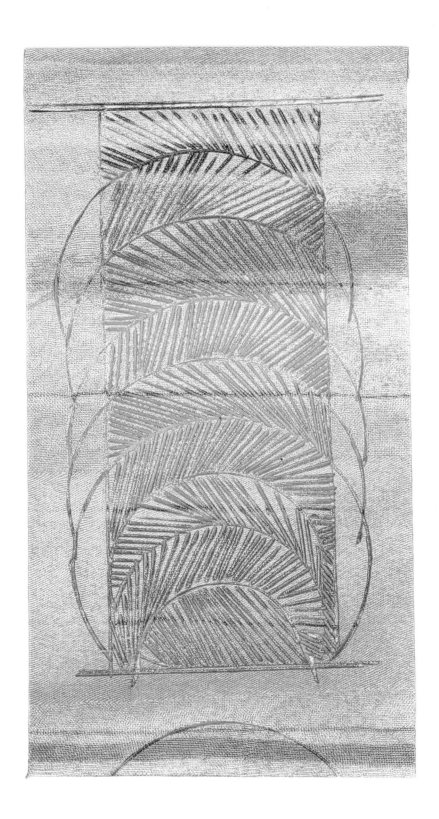

Above
A sample created using finely scored lines.

Far left
Several layers of lightweight patterned fabric on a base of nylon organza have been scored with straight lines and cross-hatching marks.

Cutting

Don't think of the soldering iron simply as a useful pair of scissors. It is so much more: cutting synthetic fabrics with scissors is fine, but cutting with the soldering iron has the added advantage of sealing the edges and preventing any further fraying.

Working freehand

I recommend 'doodling' with the soldering iron on the fabric, because it's a good way to get a feel for how it will behave when cutting out shapes freehand. Try cutting out small shapes and creating patterns; the edges will be perfectly sealed, preventing any possibility of fraying. The secret is that the fabric must not move on the glass while the tip of the soldering iron melts and cuts through it. Nylon organza often adheres to the glass when it melts, but try not to disturb it, as this can be a great help.

Method
1. Take two pieces of organza and place them on the glass, one on top of the other. Try to hold the fabrics under some tension to prevent them from slipping about on the piece of glass.
2. Positioning the tip of the soldering iron at quite an upright angle, move it slowly and in a continuous movement. You will feel the fabrics sticking to the glass; try not to disturb them.
3. Practise cutting wavy strips, shapes and spirals (see diagram below).
4. Practise cutting out small circles, ovals and other shapes.

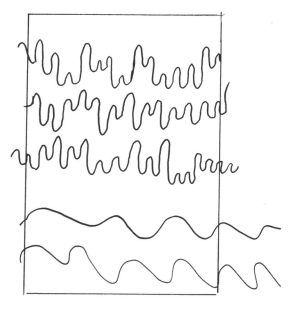

Further suggestion
- Interleave nylon organza with other synthetic fabrics.

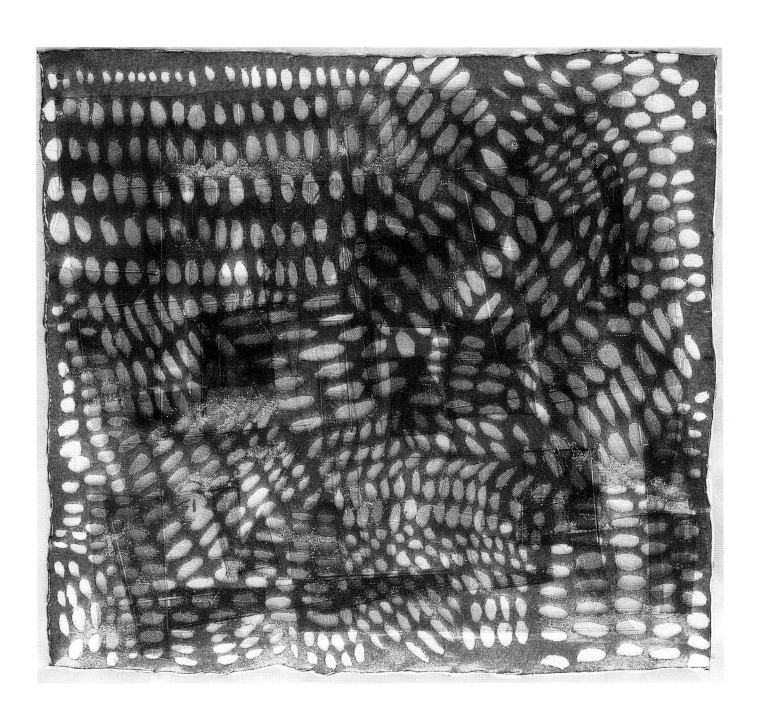

Above
Oval-shaped holes were cut into a slinky, iridescent polyester organza, which was placed over blocks of coloured organza on shiny white foil fabric.

Using metal templates

Metal templates can be used to cut out shapes and motifs. Over the years, I have assembled a large collection of interesting metal shapes. Badges, buttons, medals, coins and earrings are all very useful. Shapes or motifs cut around a template will have very neat and permanently sealed edges.

It is very important to hold the template firmly on the fabric. The pressure will prevent the fabric from moving and avoid any splits or gaps appearing when you seal two or more fabrics together. Be very careful: metal templates can get hot. The smaller the template, the greater the risk of burning your fingers!

Method

1. Place one piece of nylon organza on the glass. Cover this with an even layer of small pieces of nylon organza, in a variety of colours, and cover these with a second piece of organza.
2. Holding a template firmly on the fabric, position the tip of the soldering iron at the edge of the template at quite an upright angle and slowly move all around. Try to do this in as continuous a movement as possible to obtain a smooth clean-cut edge. The cut shape or motif will pop out easily.

Further suggestions

• Paper templates can also be used: try tracing the outlines below.

  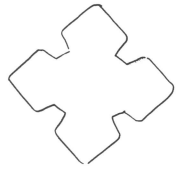

Left
Motifs, shapes and negative shapes cut using metal templates.

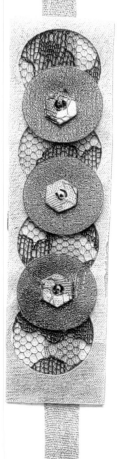

Bonding

Bonding two fabrics together usually requires an adhesive. Bondaweb is the type that is most often used, but it stiffens the fabric and makes transparent fabrics opaque. The soldering iron, however, will bond two or more fabrics together while allowing them to maintain their quality and transparency.

Bonding motifs to a ground fabric

The shapes or motifs cut in the method on page 33 may be bonded to a ground fabric.

Method
1. Take two pieces of organza and place them on the glass, one on top of the other.
2. Place a motif or shape on the pieces of organza. Press the edge of the mirror plate firmly across the centre of the motif and make a short mark with the tip of the soldering iron, as shown in the diagram below.
3. Alternatively, place the motif on the fabric and cover it with the template you used to cut it out. Very lightly run the tip of the soldering iron around the edge of the template, just enough for the edge of the motif to bond to the ground fabric.

Above left
This long piece, which could be used as a bracelet or choker, was made by bonding motifs to a ground fabric.

Right
This sample was cut through a metal grid with diamond-shaped holes, leaving a tiny area uncut at the base of each shape. The flaps were then folded back and bonded down with small bonding marks.

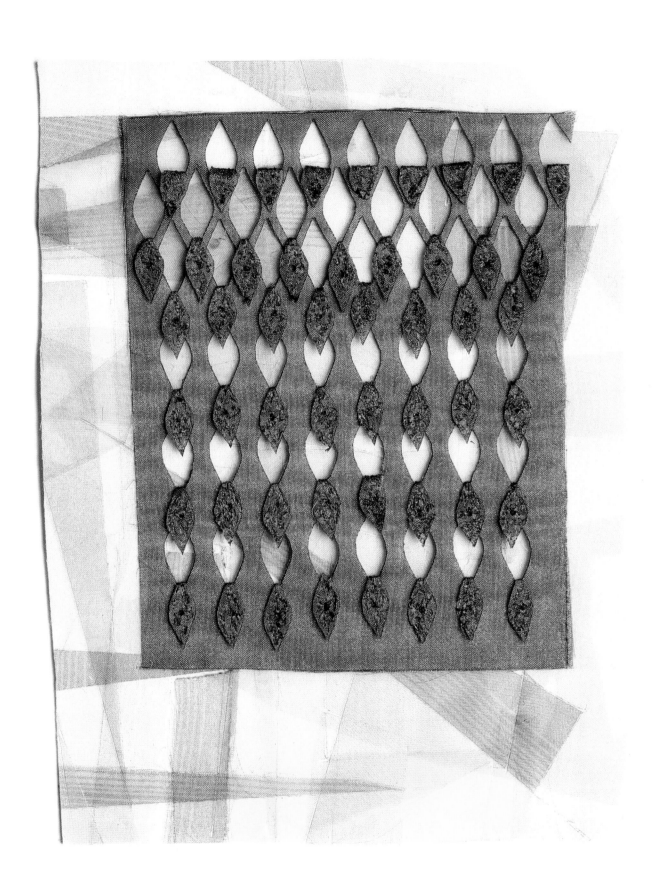

Sealing items between fabrics

Choose small flat items, such as lace, paper, leaves, petals, snippets of fabric, threads, buttons, beads or sequins, and trap them between two layers of transparent fabric.

Method
1. Place one piece of organza on the glass; place the item to be sealed on the organza, and cover with a second piece of organza.
2. Placing the ruler on the fabric, cut and seal all four sides of the fabrics, taking care to avoid touching the item with the soldering iron.

Further suggestion
• Using a very fine, sharp-tipped soldering iron, it is possible to bond multiple layers of lightweight synthetic fabric together, which can be one way of using up the more uninteresting lightweight synthetic fabrics. Use templates or a ruler as a cutting edge to cut and bond the fabrics together. In the process, they will compress and the cut edge will look rather like plywood or strata. If you have an extremely sharp tip on your soldering iron, it is possible to bond and cut through very many layers.

Left and right
Snippets of synthetic fabric were sandwiched between two pieces of nylon organza. A flower-shaped template was then used to cut out the shape. The resulting fabric, complete with its flower-shaped aperture, was bonded to another piece of nylon organza. The flower motif was then bonded in the centre of the aperture. Several similar squares were made, then pieced together with a bonded seam to give a chequered effect.

Scrunchy-textured surfaces

Try experimenting with bonding techniques to create textured surfaces. For this sample, you will require a standard-size piece of acrylic felt and two pieces of nylon organza of the same size, plus four or five pieces of nylon organza in contrasting colours, cut up into snippets, and a medium-sized tapestry needle. The easiest way to cut the snippets is to layer all the fabrics together and, using scissors, cut them into strips, then hold a layer of strips and cut across them at an angle.

Method

1. Place the felt on the glass; cover it with one of the pieces of organza, and then scatter the snippets thickly over it to make a deep mosaic of colour.
2. Cover the snippets with the remaining piece of organza.
3. Place a ruler flat on the work and run the tip of the soldering iron along the edge to mark a grid of nine squares. This will bond the layers together at the same time.
4. In one of the squares, very lightly stroke over the surface of the fabric with the tip of the soldering iron. Put no pressure on the fabrics at all and give the fabrics time to melt, allowing the colours to blend together to form quite a firm, scrunchy surface.
5. Move to another square, insert the tapestry needle underneath the top layer and lift it to create space between the snippets and the top layer. Melt cracks and holes in the surface fabric by touching on the needle with the soldering iron and into the space created between the snippets and the top layer. Don't rush this, as it takes time for the melted edges to harden and for the cracks and holes to develop crisp scrunchy edges. The needle protects the snippets beneath from being touched by the soldering iron. Take the needle out and reinsert it in other areas. If you do not clean the tip of the soldering iron too often, you will get a lovely dark tinge on the edge of the cracks and holes, which looks good.
6. Experiment in the other squares, combining scrunchy textures with mark-making, scoring lines and patterning.

Right
A series of samples made by combining scrunchy-textured surfaces with mark-making.

A grid was scored on the fabric, using a metal grid as a template. The top layer of organza has been removed from some of the squares, and the fabrics beneath have been textured and marked with simple patterns and embellished with hand stitching.

USING A METAL GRID

Try using a metal grid instead of a ruler to mark out your design. This very strong metal grid is sold in garden centres or DIY shops and is sold in quite large sheets. Wear protective gloves and use wire cutters to cut a piece with five squares each way.

Method

1. Holding the grid firmly on the fabrics, run the tip of the soldering iron along both sides of every bar to score a grid pattern on the fabric, at the same time as bonding all the layers together.
2. Make marks and texture in the squares.

Using up waste scraps

Waste scraps and strips of synthetic fabric can be bonded together with the soldering iron to make a new and textured fabric.

Method
1. Place a base piece of organza on the glass and layer lots of waste fabric pieces on top. This can be done randomly or in a more considered way.
2. Place a ruler on the layered scraps and run the tip of the soldering iron lightly along the edge.
3. Repeat this process over the whole surface until the fabric holds together in one piece.

Further suggestions
• Place a metal template on top of layered scraps. Run the tip of the soldering iron around the template to cut out textured shapes or motifs.
• Place an intricately cut metal stencil on top of layered waste fabric. Run the tip of the soldering iron through the slits and patterns of the stencil to bond the fabrics together.

Right
Strips of waste fabric bonded together to make colourful new fabric.

Advanced techniques

You have now learned the three basic techniques: mark-making, cutting and bonding. Once you feel more confident with the soldering iron, you can start to combine these techniques to create innovative and beautiful effects. The following advanced techniques give some starting points for further experimentation.

Removing selected areas

It takes a little practice with this technique before you know just how deeply to score into the felt with the soldering iron. Once again, a medium-sized tapestry needle makes a useful tool for separating fabrics.

Method 1

1. Place a piece of acrylic felt on the glass and cover it with a piece of nylon organza.
2. Use the soldering iron to score a grid pattern over the fabric layers, using the width of the ruler as a guide for size.
3. Insert the tapestry needle under the organza in one of the squares, pushing it as close as possible to the bonding line.
4. Give a little push upwards with the needle to break the seal between the organza and the felt and carefully peel off one square of organza. Hold down the edge of the adjacent square to prevent it too from lifting off the felt. Remove more squares in the same way.

Method 2

For this technique, you will also need a metal template, not too intricate in shape.
1. Holding the template firmly on the work, run the tip of the soldering iron at a fairly upright angle around the edge to mark and score the shape, scoring not too deeply into the felt.
2. Repeat two or three more times, making sure there is a good gap between the shapes.
3. Carefully remove the fabric surrounding the shapes, holding them down with your fingers to prevent them from lifting. It can be helpful to place the template back on the shape when you do this. You may also find the tapestry needle useful for breaking the seal between the organza and the felt (see above).

Further suggestion
- If you are careful, it is often possible to remove a layer or layers with your fingers.

Top right
Scoring around a template and removing shapes or background fabric.

Bottom right
A mosaic of nylon organza was layered onto acrylic felt then covered with a single piece of nylon organza. A grid pattern was scored and selected areas of the top layer were removed.

Scoring patterns using metal templates

Before experimenting with this method, it may be helpful to practice drawing on paper around the template to create patterns. Choose an acrylic felt in a strong colour and three pieces of nylon organza, the same size, in colours that will contrast with the felt.

Method

1. Put the felt on the glass and layer the three pieces of organza on top.
2. Holding the template firmly on the fabrics, run the tip of the soldering iron around the template or part of the template. The tip will melt into the fabric and make a mark at the same time as bonding the organzas to the felt. Be careful not to score too heavily or you will cut through to the glass. Move the template over the fabric to create an interesting design all over it (the diagram below left gives some ideas).

Further suggestions

- Sandwich snippets of synthetic fabric between acrylic felt and nylon organza and then score the design.
- Create scrunchy-textured areas within the design (see page 38).
- Embellish with machine or hand stitching.
- Try removing selected layers. See page 42.

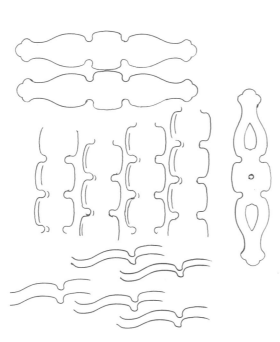

Far right
This pattern was scored over and over using a metal template.

Above
A grid was scored on a mosaic of polyester organza and acrylic felt, then marks were made within the squares using templates.

Mark-making, cutting and bonding   45

Fancy borders

Using this technique, it is possible to cut and bond the edges of two pieces of fabric together in one action. When cutting a number of strips you may find that the strips will adhere to the glass. This can be very helpful, so try not to disturb them until the last strip has been cut.

Method 1

1. Place two pieces of nylon organza on the glass, one on top of the other.
2. Place the ruler on the fabrics and hold it firmly to prevent them from slipping.
3. Slowly run the tip of the soldering iron along the edge of the ruler, as if drawing a line with a pencil. The two fabrics will bond together and the excess fabric will be cut away at the same time.
4. Leave the ruler in position and carefully remove the excess fabric. To ensure a perfect bond with no gaps, it will sometimes be necessary to tilt and press the edge of the ruler very firmly on the fabrics. The amount of pressure required will often depend on the type of fabric, or the number of layers being used.
5. Cut out a number of strips of various widths.
6. Place a strip horizontally on the glass, making sure that it lies flat.
7. Place a coin or other template on the strip. Pressing your finger firmly on the coin and holding the soldering iron at an upright angle, slowly run the tip halfway around the edge to form a scallop. Slide the coin along and cut another scallop, linking it with the previous one. Continue along the rest of the strip, forming a scalloped edge all along the length. See the diagram below for some ideas.
8. Practice using different shapes of template and widths of strip.

Further suggestion
- Try cutting fancy borders freehand.

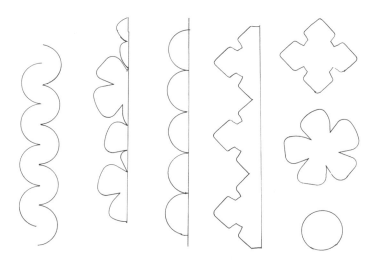

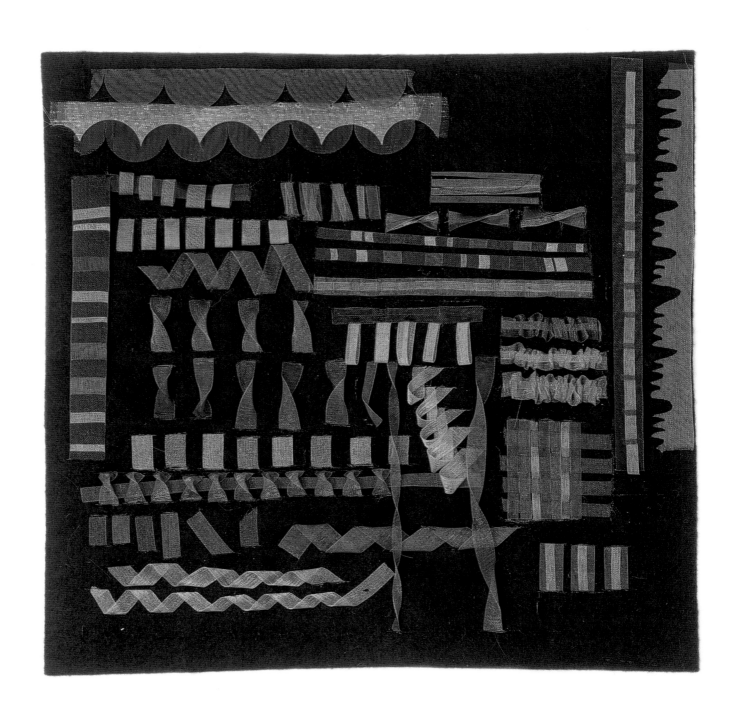

Above
Fancy borders and strips in various
colours of nylon organza were bonded
to a base layer of black acrylic felt.

Above
Fancy borders have been lightly bonded to a
base fabric of nylon organza.

Right
Fancy borders layered on top of one another.

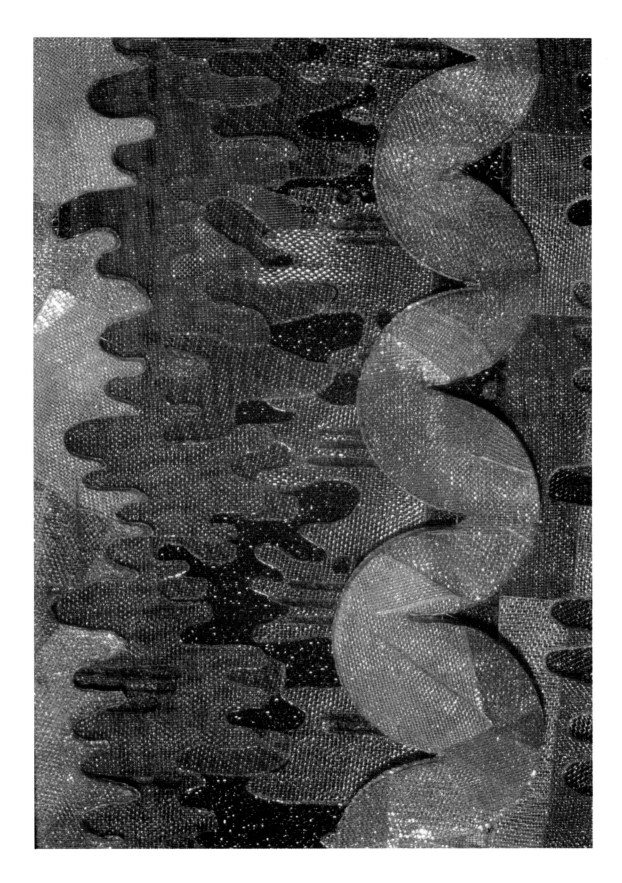

Method 2

1. Place a strip 4cm (1½in) wide, cut using the method described previously, on the glass and squash it so that the top and bottom sealed edges are now centre front and back.
2. Place a template or coin on the strip. Cut halfway around the template and then repeat along the length of the strip.
3. Repeat the pattern on the bottom edge of the strip (see diagram below).

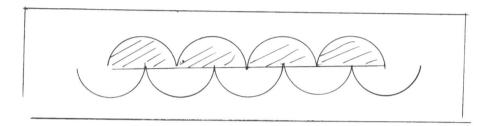

Method 3

1. Place a fancy-edged strip, on top of a straight-edged one, horizontally on the glass, as shown in the diagram above.
2. Place the ruler flat on the strips, vertically. Run the tip of the soldering iron down the ruler to bond the strips together and cut through them. Cut the rest of the strip into pieces varying from 2 to 4cm (¾ to 1½in) in width, and put them to one side.
3. Place a piece of acrylic felt on the glass. Take one of the cut pieces and place it on the felt.
4. Position the edge of the ruler on the very edge of the cut piece. Run the tip of the soldering iron lightly along the ruler, with just enough pressure to bond the edge of the piece to the felt. Bond around all four sides, and then bond the remaining pieces to the felt in the same way.

Right
EXHIBITION MANIA
The original design for this piece was traced onto a polyester organza backing fabric. Strips of nylon organza were layered and bonded onto the backing fabric. The design was free-machine embroidered from the back of the work (Photograph: Andrew Smart).

Hollow 3-D shapes

The finished shapes made with this technique look like little pillows.

Method
1.   Take a strip of nylon or organza measuring approximately 6 x 14cm (2½ x 5½in) and lay it horizontally on the glass.
2.   Fold the strip in half from bottom to top, and align the edges.
3.   Position the edge of the ruler about 5mm (¼in) from the aligned edges.
4.   Pressing the ruler firmly on the fabric, run the tip of the soldering iron along the edge to seal the two edges together.
5.   Leave the ruler in position and remove the excess fabric. Run the tip of the iron along the edge of the ruler again, to reinforce the seal. You now have a hollow tube of fabric.
6.   Place the tube vertically on the glass and squash it so that the seam is centre front.
7.   To cut and seal the top of the tube, tilt and press the edge of the mirror plate firmly on the tube, about 5mm (¼in) from the top. Run the tip of the soldering iron along the edge. Leave the mirror plate in position and remove the excess fabric. Reinforce the seal by running the tip along the sealed edge a second time.
8.   Turn the tube around so that the sealed end is at the bottom of the glass.
9.   Place the edge of the mirror plate about 3cm (1¼in) up from the sealed end of the tube. As you do this, give a little backwards push with the mirror plate to push air inside the tube. Cut and seal as before. Leaving the ruler in position, remove the excess fabric. Reinforce the seal as before.
10. Repeat from 7 to 9 along the length of the tube.

Hollow Humbug Shapes
1.   Follow the previous instructions from 1 to 7 to make a tube and seal one end of it.
2.   Turn the tube so that the sealed edge is at the bottom of the glass.
3.   Squash the tube so that the long sealed seam is facing the left-hand side of the glass.
4.   Place the edge of the ruler about 3.5cm (1½in) up from the sealed end of the tube. Cut and seal.
5.   Reinforce the seal a second time. The hollow humbug shape should now have two perfectly sealed ends.
6.   Cut and seal the rest of the tube in the same way.

Further suggestions
•   Before sealing the final edge of the hollow shapes, trap items such as small beads, threads or fabric inside.
•   Make shapes of different sizes by altering the width and length of the tube.
•   Try using synthetic fabrics of varying weights and textures. You will find some fabrics bond or cut more easily than others.

Above
3-D hollow shapes made with patchwork samples.

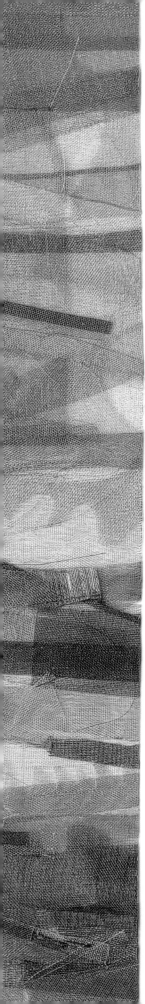

Patchwork techniques

The following methods are based on traditional patchwork techniques. You will be amazed by the neatness of the seams you can achieve using the soldering iron.

Piecing strips together

To make this sample, you will need several colours of nylon organza, cut into strips ranging from 3 to 5cm (1¼ to 2 in) wide x 12cm (4¾ in) long. The easiest way to cut the strips is to layer the fabrics one on top of the other and use scissors to cut them into strips.

Method

1. Place two strips of contrasting colours, one on top of the other, horizontally on the glass.
2. Holding the ruler firmly on the fabrics, 3mm (⅛ in) below the top edge of the strips, run the tip of the soldering iron slowly along to bond the edges together.
3. Keeping the ruler in position, gently remove the excess fabric.
4. Lift off the ruler and carefully open out the fabric; the strips will be joined with a perfect seam.
5. Press lightly along the seam with your finger to flatten it. Do not turn the work over when bonding on consecutive strips.
6. Take a third strip and align the edge of this strip with the top edge of the second strip.
7. Holding the ruler firmly on the fabrics, 3mm (⅛ in) below the aligned edges, run the tip of the soldering iron slowly along the edge of the ruler to bond the strips together. Keep the ruler in position and gently remove the excess fabric.
8. Open out the fabrics and gently flatten the seam. You now have three strips seamed together, forming one piece.
9. Repeat the process until you have pieced together several strips. Don't worry about the waste produced when bonding strips together as you can save these scraps to be used later.

Right

Top: Castellated pleats made by bonding two seams, turning the work over and bonding two more seams, and repeating this process several times.
Centre and bottom: Concertina pleats made by turning the work over every time a new strip is bonded.

Intricate patchwork patterns

You could use the striped sample made in the previous method for the following technique, which is based on traditional Seminole patchwork. Strips of fabric are pieced together and then cut up into strips. The strips are then pieced back together again. Very intricate patchwork patterns can be made by piecing and cutting several times.

Method

1. Place the striped fabric on the glass, with the stripes facing you vertically.
2. Place the ruler flat on the fabric, 1cm (³⁄₈in) from the top edge, and run the tip of the soldering iron along the edge to neaten and remove any frayed edges.
3. Place the ruler on the fabric horizontally and slide it down to cut strips varying from 3 to 5cm (1¼ to 2in) wide. If the fabric adheres to the glass, try not to disturb it until the last strip has been cut.
4. Lift the strips carefully off the glass, trying to keep them all right side up.
5. Place one strip horizontally on the glass.
6. Take a second strip and place it on top of the first strip, aligning the top edges but slightly offsetting the colours.

Below
Strips have been cut and pieced to form blocks of colour.

7. Placing the ruler 5mm (¼in) away from the top edge of the strips, run the tip of the soldering iron along the edge to cut and seal the strips together. Carefully remove the excess fabric.
8. Fold open the strips and gently press along the seam with your finger to flatten it.

9. Continue bonding all the strips, one after the other, offsetting the colours to make a whole piece.
10. Cut the whole piece into diagonal strips with the soldering iron, rearrange them and bond them back together again.
11. There will be a limit to the number of times you can keep cutting and re-bonding the strips. This will depend on the strength of the original fabric and the width of the strips that were originally cut. The bonded seams are quite strong, but handle them with care.
12. Save all the excess narrow waste strips to use later.

Note that soft, flimsy, loosely woven fabrics may not lie flat when seamed together: they tend to form into soft folds.

Further suggestions

- Bond strips together at an angle rather than horizontally.
- Bond plain strips between patchwork strips.
- Use patchwork for cutting fancy borders and ribbons.
- Use for mark-making and cutting out shapes using templates.
- Use patchwork for 3D hollow forms.
- Bond strips to form the traditional patchwork log cabin pattern.
- Bond one patchwork piece over another piece.

Below left
Strips that have been cut and pieced several times.

Below right
Strips that have been seamed at an angle.

Patchwork strips and ribbons

The technique described below uses the waste strips produced using previously described techniques to make strips or ribbons with crossbars bonded to them, rather like the rungs of ladders.

Method

1. Lay a base of nylon organza on the glass. Position the waste strips vertically on the organza, leaving gaps of approximately 1cm (³⁄₈in) between strips.
2. Place the metal ruler horizontally on the strips, 5mm (¼in) from the top of the fabric (see diagram below left).
3. Slowly move the tip of the soldering iron along the edge of the ruler. This will bond the waste strips to the ground fabric, at the same time neatening any frayed edges. Leave the ruler in position and remove the excess fabric.
4. Slide the ruler down and cut the entire fabric into strips (see diagram below right).

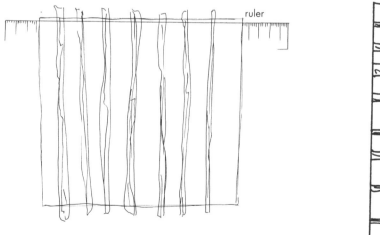

Above
Using both the patchwork method described on page 56
and the waste scraps method on page 41, strips 4cm (1½in) wide
were cut, rearranged and bonded back together again.
Very narrow patchwork strips were laid across
the surface and sealed to the edges of the work.

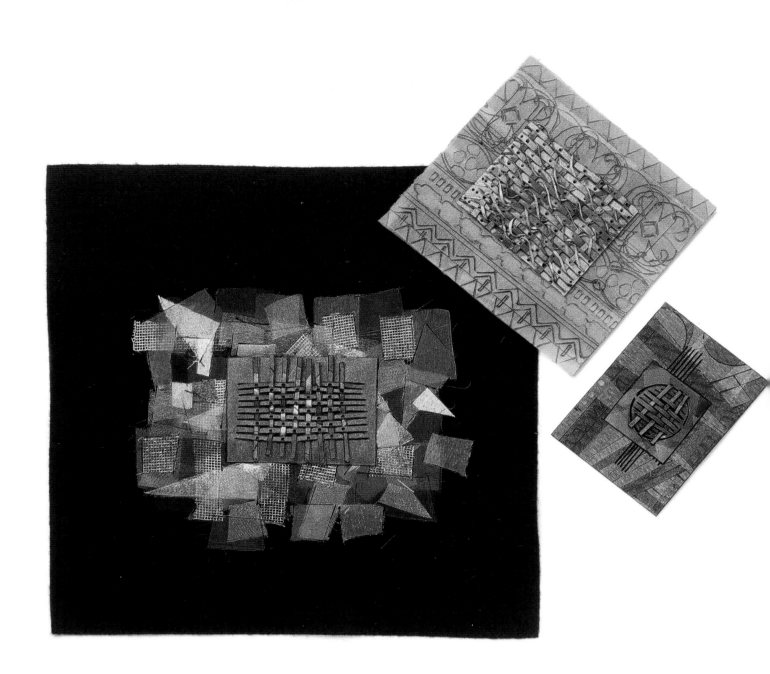

Above

Parallel vertical slits were cut into the centre of the fabric to form a warp. The weft strips were cut from a contrasting fabric and woven through the slits. Small bonding marks were made where the warp and weft crossed over.

Mark-making, cutting and bonding   61

Design workshop: mosaic sample

The next section gives instructions on making a sample piece that combines many of the techniques you have learnt so far. The aim is to consolidate your knowledge of soldering iron techniques before you go on to the techniques in the rest of the book. Step-by-step methods are given for each stage of working. My original sample was based on a contemporary stained-glass mosaic, and I have shown it in different colourways to show the varied effects that can be achieved.

Stage 1 Making the sample

This stage uses simple mark-making, including eyelets, to create the basis of the sample. You will require a standard-sized piece of acrylic felt in a strong colour, five pieces of nylon organza in different colours, cut into a variety of shapes and sizes, and a few small snippets of iridescent polyester organza or other contrasting lightweight glitzy fabric (the fabric should be non-stretchy). For this method, a mirror plate makes an ideal and practical small ruler.

Method
1. Place the felt on the glass and cover it with two or three layers of the organza shapes, overlapping them to form a mosaic of colour and adding a few small pieces of iridescent organza or other contrasting fabric to give highlights.
2. Run the tip of the soldering iron along the edge of the mirror plate to bond the organza shapes to the felt and to score strong lines.
3. Make marks and patterns all over the mosaic, as shown in the diagram below.

Far right
Stage 1 of the sample: mark-making techniques.

Stage 2 Cutting out shapes

Using a mirror plate and a coin or another simple template, the mosaic sample can then be cut into shapes.

Method

1. Place the sample on the glass.
2. To cut out squares, rectangles and triangles, approximately 3 to 4 cm (1¼ to 1½in) in size, tilt and press the edge of the mirror plate firmly on the work and then slowly run the tip of the soldering iron along the edge, holding it at a fairly upright angle. Make sure that the tip of the soldering iron cuts right through the fabric to the glass. To cut out a circle, press a coin on the fabric and work around the edge.
3. The cut shapes should pop out easily with a little push from the back. See the diagram below for some ideas.

Far right
Stage 2: cutting out shapes. Also shows frames (see stage 5, page 70).

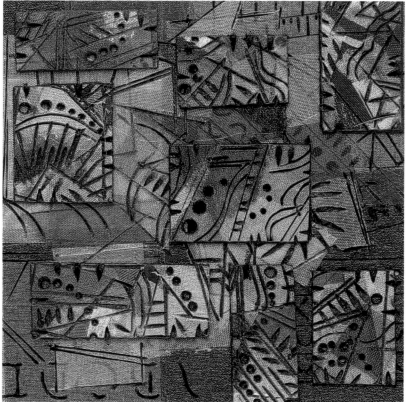

Top and bottom
Stage 3: bonding
cut shapes to a
base fabric.

Stage 3 Appliqué

The cut shapes produced in the previous sample can then be bonded back onto the original sample, as here, or to some other piece of your choice.

Method

1. Place the mosaic sample, which now has apertures cut into it, on the glass.
2. Place a shape on the sample; press the tip of the soldering iron sideways onto its edge, and let it melt through all the layers into the backing felt. This will make a small triangular mark as it bonds the shape to the sample. Repeat this randomly around the edge of the shape, varying the size of the triangular marks by adjusting how much of the tip overlaps the edge of the shape (see diagram below).
3. If you prefer not to see the bonding marks, hold the shape in place and carefully turn the work over. Feel for the position of the shape and press the tip of the soldering iron sideways into it, pressing deeply enough to bond the two layers together.

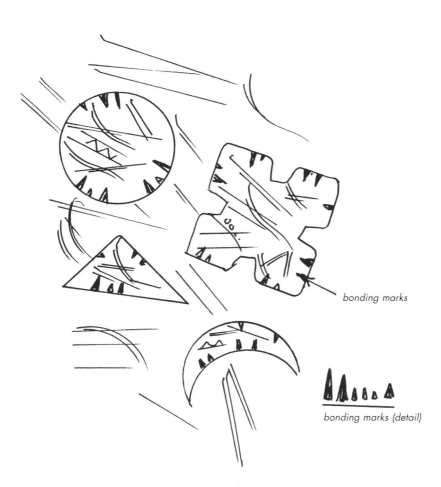

bonding marks

bonding marks (detail)

Stage 4 Bonding fabric over apertures

The apertures left by the cut shapes can now be backed with nylon organza.

Method

1. Place the work face down on the glass and cover an aperture with a piece of nylon organza. Make sure that the organza overlaps the edges of the aperture by at least 1cm (³⁄₈in).
2. Tilt and press the ruler or mirror plate on to the organza (diagram A below).
3. Run the tip of the soldering iron lightly along the edge of the ruler or mirror plate to bond the organza to the felt around all sides of the aperture. Bond organza over the rest of the apertures, using a different colour for each one if you wish.
4. Place the edge of the ruler or mirror plate back onto the bonding line and carefully tear away the excess fabric. Sometimes it can be easily lifted away without using the ruler or mirror plate. The result on the rear side of the sample can be seen in diagram B below.

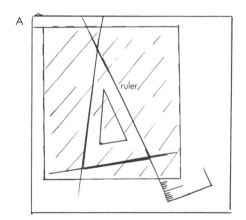
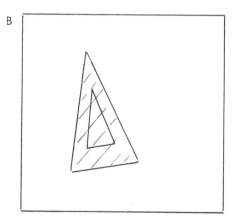

Left
Stages 4 and 5: organza has been bonded to the back of all the apertures in this stage of the sample. Some of the organza-backed apertures have been developed into frames (see stage 5).

Stage 5 Cutting out frames

Once the apertures in the sample have been backed with organza, you can cut them out to make little fabric frames, also with organza backing. These can then be manipulated and bonded back to the sample itself, or to other pieces.

Method

1. Place the work right side up on the glass and position the ruler or mirror plate about 5mm (¼in) away from the edge of an aperture that has been backed with organza. Tilt the edge of the ruler or mirror plate towards the aperture.
2. Placing the tip of the soldering iron on the edge of the ruler or mirror plate, slowly cut around all sides of the aperture, cutting right through to the glass. A framed shape with an organza backing will pop out.
3. Develop this by leaving one corner of the frame uncut. This will enable it to be twisted, repositioned and bonded back onto the sample.
4. Position the tip of the soldering iron sideways onto the border of the frame and press it through all the layers into the backing felt; you need only make one or two of these bonding marks.
5. Finally, turn the work over and bond a piece of organza in a contrasting colour over the new aperture, as in stage 4.

Further suggestion

- Combine other synthetic fabrics, such as glitzy lamé and nets, at stage 1.

Right
Sample showing shapes cut and bonded back on, plus apertures and frames backed with nylon organza.

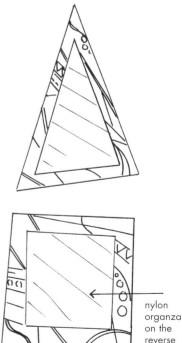

nylon organza on the reverse side

Project: a fabric book

Here, mountboard is sealed between fabrics to make a book cover with ribbon ties.

Requirements
- Two pieces of mountboard, measuring 9 × 12cm (3½ × 4¾in)
- Metal safety ruler (this is the ideal tool for this technique)
- A decorative fabric on a base of acrylic felt, measuring 24 × 16cm (9½ × 5½in), for the outer side of the cover (you could use one of the mark-making techniques to make the fabric for the front of the cover)
- A piece of synthetic fabric, thinner than acrylic felt, and to the same measurements as the above, for the lining
- Two narrow ribbons (to match the cover), 5mm (¼in) wide and 15cm (6in) long (see Strips and fancy borders, page 46)

Method
1. Place the lining fabric right side down on the glass.
2. Place the two pieces of mountboard level in the middle of the fabric, leaving a 5mm (¼in) gap between them.
3. Making sure that the gap stays the same, place the front cover fabric right side up over the two pieces of board.
4. Place the safety ruler horizontally on the fabric, 3cm (1¼in) below the top edge of both pieces of board.
5. Carefully slide the ruler up the fabric until you feel it slip over the edge of the board.
6. Press your fingers firmly in the ridge of the ruler and pull back on it to make sure it butts up against the mountboard.
7. Place the tip of the soldering iron on the edge of the ruler, 2cm (¾in) to the left of the mountboard. Cut and seal along the ruler, 2cm (¾in) beyond the other end of the mountboard, and remove the excess fabric.
8. Turning the work so that the bottom edge now faces the top of the glass, cut and seal it in the same way.

Ribbon ties
1. To seal the ties to the sides of the covers, lay a ribbon horizontally across the centre of the work, with the outside cover fabric facing you, so that one end overlaps the unsealed right-hand side of the cover by from 2 to 3cm (¼ to 1in).

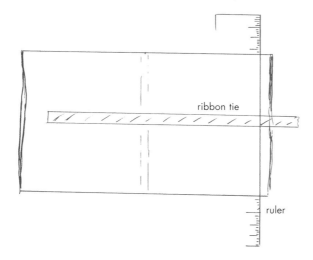

ribbon tie

ruler

2. Placing the safety ruler vertically on the ribbon, slide it to the right until you feel it slip over the mountboard (see diagram on page 70). Make sure the edge of the ruler butts up close to the board.
3. Run the tip of the soldering iron down the edge of the ruler to cut and seal the side of the cover; the ribbon will be sealed on the side at the same time.

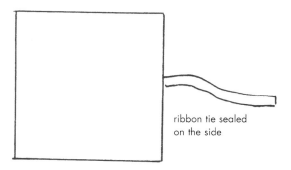

ribbon tie sealed
on the side

4. Turn the work so that the remaining unsealed edge is on the right-hand side.
5. Repeat steps 1–3 to cut and seal the side with the second ribbon.
6. Fold in the middle.

Fixing the pages
Fabric pages can now be inserted into the cover.

1. Take five pieces of acrylic felt. Cut the first piece 1cm (³⁄₈in) smaller all around than the size of the open book cover. Cut each of the remaining four pieces 1cm (³⁄₈in) smaller all round each time. Also cut a length of ribbon from the same fabric used for the front cover.
2. Open out the book cover and place it right side down on the glass.
3. Starting with the largest piece, layer the pieces of felt on the lining.
4. Feel for the centre fold of the cover and push the tip of the soldering iron through all the layers to make an eyelet. The tip should just about reach through and make a mark on the other side. Make an even number of holes, spaced out along the fold (see diagram on opposite page). Turn the work over and push the tip through on the marks to complete the eyelets.
5. Thread the strip of ribbon through a very large-eyed needle or bodkin and run it through the eyelets. Seal and cut off any excess ribbon.

Far right
Book covers made
with decorative
mark-making
techniques.
My thanks to
Cindy Rose.

Further suggestions
• Use hand-made paper instead of felt for the pages. You may have to extend the width of the spine to allow for more pages.
• The method for fixing ribbon ties can easily be adapted to bond loops onto the edges of fabric.

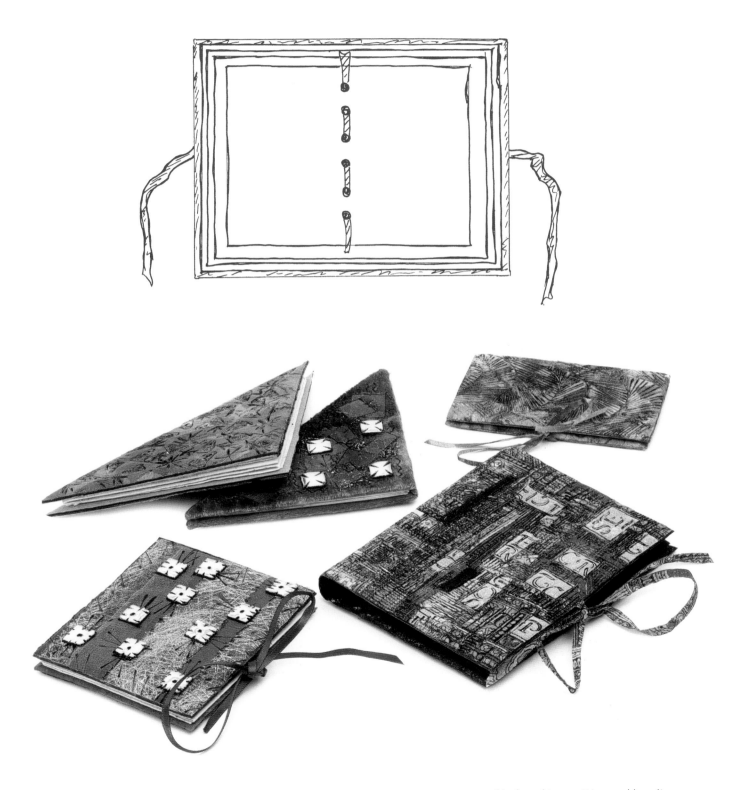

CHAPTER TWO
MACHINE STITCHING

Combining soldering iron techniques with machine stitching can give very effective results. Always test your threads before you start to stitch, because the thread will come into contact with the soldering iron and you don't want the stitching to melt away. Natural threads, such as cotton, silk and good-quality rayon, are ideal. Metallic threads should be tested first. To test thread, hold a length under tension on the glass and run the tip of the soldering iron across it two or three times. If the thread melts, don't use it.

The easiest way to stitch on lightweight fabric is to stretch the fabric in a hoop, then free-machine your design. If you have never tried this technique, you will find that there are lots of beautifully illustrated books on the subject, written by very well-known authors. Before consulting these, however, look in your sewing machine instruction manual for the basic technique as it relates to your machine.

Stitched motifs

It takes time and patience to machine stitch a motif or a design onto synthetic fabric and then cut it out with scissors. It is almost impossible to achieve without some whiskers of frayed edges showing. You will find that cutting around stitched borders with the soldering iron can be done very quickly and easily, and this technique has the added advantage of permanently sealing the edges, preventing any frayed edges spoiling the effect. It beats using scissors by a long way!

For this sample you will require two pieces of nylon organza, plus scraps in a variety of colours cut into small pieces. You will also need machine embroidery threads. These should be tested first, as described above, to check that they will not melt. For free-machine embroidery, the fabric is held in an embroidery hoop, which should be prepared by binding the inner hoop with bias binding, to avoid the fabric slipping.

Method
1. Sandwich a layer of small pieces of nylon organza, in various colours, between the two larger pieces of organza and stretch them in an embroidery hoop.
2. Free-machine simple motifs or shapes.
3. Placing the hoop with the fabric touching the glass, position the tip of the soldering iron right against the edge of the stitching and run it all the way around each motif. The motifs will neatly pop out.

Left
Polyester organza fragments were sandwiched between two pieces of polyester organza. A motif was stitched and cut out with the soldering iron.
My thanks to Clare Muir.

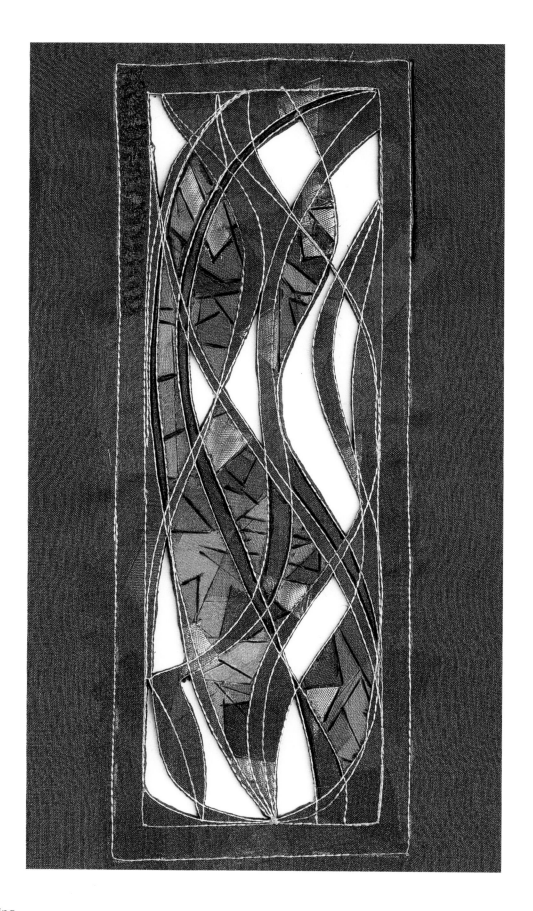

Cutwork

This method is based on traditional cutwork, in which parts of the background fabric, or the negative areas, are cut out. It can be highly effective, leading to very intricate and lacy finished pieces. It is very important to ensure that all the stitching links together to prevent any areas of the work falling apart when the selected areas are cut out.

Method
1. Layer three pieces of nylon organza, one on top of the other, and stretch them in the hoop.
2. Stitch a simple design, making sure that all areas link together. See diagram below for one suggestion, in which a motif is repeated.
3. To cut out the selected areas, place the work on the glass and position the tip of the soldering iron right against the stitching. Move it slowly all around the edge and the cut areas will neatly pop out.

Further suggestions
*   Stitch or carefully bond a piece of organza in a contrasting colour to the back of the work, over the cut-out areas.
*   Trace or draw the design on the fabric first.
*   Remove selected layers of fabric (see page 82).

Left
Cutwork sample showing selected areas
cut out with the soldering iron.

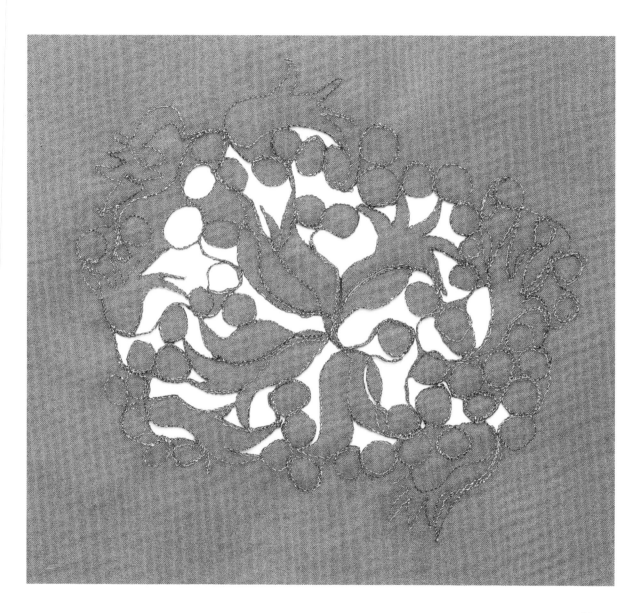

Above
A simple cutwork design was stitched onto three layers of organza and selected areas were then cut out.

Right
TREAD SOFTLY
This cutwork panel was kindly loaned by Shirley Baldwin (photograph by Andrew Smart).

Appliqué

This method is based on traditional appliqué, in which motifs cut from one fabric are stitched to a background fabric. The edges of the applied fabric are usually neatened in some way to prevent them from fraying. In this method, the excess fabric is cut away with the soldering iron at the very edge of the stitching. Here, a range of synthetic fabrics, such as net, chiffon, organza and polyester, are applied to a background of felt.

Method
1. Place a piece of synthetic fabric on the felt and machine a simple shape or motif in the centre of it. There is no need to stretch the felt in a hoop, as the felt is quite firm.
2. To remove the excess fabric surrounding the stitching, place the work on the glass and lift an edge of the top fabric, holding it very taut. Cut in from the edge with the soldering iron until you reach the stitching. Keeping the fabric taut, move the tip quickly around the very edge of the stitching until the excess top fabric has been cut away.
3. Using a variety of fabrics, continue stitching motifs, and removing the excess fabric. Layer and overlap the motifs to add depth to the finished piece.

Left and above
A range of synthetic fabrics was used to build up the layers of motifs, creating depth. The excess fabric was removed each time a motif was stitched.

Reverse appliqué

In traditional reverse appliqué, several layers of fabric are layered, one on top of the another, and stitched together. Selected layers of fabric are then cut back with very fine pointed scissors to reveal the fabrics beneath.

Reverse appliqué has always been one of my favourite techniques, and I have spent many hours using scissors to cut away layers of synthetic fabric and trying to cut off all the whiskers of frayed fabric. Initial experiments with the soldering iron soon made me realize that reverse appliqué was going to be a lot easier from now on. The soldering iron makes the process quick and easy, with the added advantage of permanently sealing all the frayed edges.

For this method, you will need to stitch a design suitable for cutwork (see page 77). The technique shown here uses a medium-sized tapestry needle in conjunction with the soldering iron to help cut back selected areas of the fabric layers from the base layer of acrylic felt. Note that the colour of the felt will have an effect on the colour of the organzas laid over it. As usual, test your embroidery threads before starting to make sure that they will not melt. A very sharp, fine-tipped soldering iron is essential for perfect results with this technique.

Method

1. Place three layers of organza, in contrasting colours, on the felt. Think carefully about the order in which you layer the colours, bearing in mind how the colours will change when selected layers are removed.
2. Stitch a simple design, suitable for cutwork, within a border.
3. Stitch again 2 to 3mm ($\frac{1}{12}$ to $\frac{1}{8}$in) away from the first line of stitching.
4. Place the work on the glass and insert the tip of the tapestry needle just underneath the surface of the top layer of fabric, very close to the stitched line.
5. Push the needle right up against the stitch line, making sure there is no gap between the needle and the stitching. The needle will prevent the layers beneath from being touched by the soldering iron and will also protect your fingers.
6. Run the tip of the soldering iron along the side of the needle and continue moving the needle all around the line of stitching. You will find that the needle will reach into the narrowest of corners.
7. Once you have a big enough flap of fabric to hold in your fingers, the needle will become redundant.
8. Cut back selected areas of the second layer of fabric in the same way to reveal the colour beneath.
9. Cut back selected areas of the third layer to reveal the colour of the felt.
10. To emphasize the design, score between the double lines of stitching with the tip of the soldering iron.

Right
Four layers of polyester organza on a base of white acrylic felt were stitched with a tulip design, then layers were removed to reveal the colours beneath. Design taken from Art Nouveau Stained Glass Pattern Book by Ed Sibbett Jr (Dover Publications).

Above
Sample showing the carved
or relief effect. The felt has been
distorted with a hot air tool.

Creating a carved or relief effect

Natural fabrics, such as silk organza or cotton organdie and some metallic fabrics, will not melt with the heat of the soldering iron. They are firm and crisp, which makes them very suitable for the backing fabric of this technique, as the soldering iron will only melt through the synthetic layers, leaving the backing fabric intact.

Method

1. Take three pieces of nylon organza, in contrasting colours, and layer them on a piece of acrylic felt, the same size. Consider the colour order of the layers of organza very carefully.
2. Place the layers of fabric on a piece of silk organza (the silk organza is behind the felt) and pin or baste all the layers together.
3. Machine stitch a cutwork design through all the layers, and again stitch a second line 2 to 3mm ($^{1}/_{12}$ to $^{1}/_{8}$ in) away from the first line of stitching.
4. To cut out the chosen areas as far as the silk organza, place the work on the glass and position the tip of the soldering iron at the side of the stitching. The tip will melt through the synthetic fabrics and stop at the silk. Move the tip slowly all around the stitching; you will feel and hear the texture of the silk as the tip of the soldering iron moves over it. Do not press too hard on the silk because a very sharp tip could score it.
5. Give a little push on the back of the silk and the cut areas will pop out leaving the silk intact.
6. In some areas, create a scrunchy-textured surface (see page 38).
7. In other areas, use the reverse appliqué technique to remove one or two layers of nylon organza (see page 82).
8. To emphasize the design, score between the double lines with the tip of the iron.

Further suggestion

•   Trace your design on the top layer of organza before you stitch.

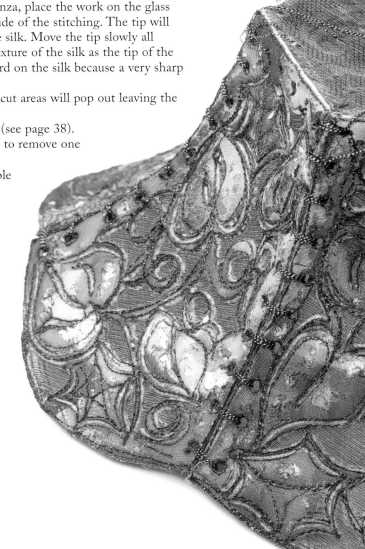

Right
LAMPSHADE
A mosaic of polyester organza was laid over white acrylic felt and placed on silk organza. A design suitable for cutwork was free-machined over the fragments. The negative areas of the design were cut back as far as the silk. Six panels were made and stitched to the frame.

Project: Mirror pocket

This design is based on cutwork and is stitched using free-machine embroidery. A mirror tile is sealed inside a pocket, the front of the pocket forming the mirror frame. The pocket is made slightly larger than the mirror tile so that the mirror will easily slip into it. A very sharp, fine-tipped soldering iron is essential for perfect results.

Requirements
- One mirror tile, measuring 13cm (5¼in) square
- A thin piece of card, measuring 14cm (5½in) square
- Two pieces of acrylic felt, standard size
- One piece of polyester organza, the same size as the felt
- Polyester organza in a variety of colours, cut into small pieces
- Machine embroidery threads (non-meltable)

Method
1. Place one piece of felt on the glass and cover it with a mosaic of small polyester organza pieces. Bond the pieces to the felt, just enough to prevent them from slipping about, and cover it with the single piece of polyester organza.
2. Place the card on the work and either very lightly run the tip of the soldering iron around its edge to make a few basting-stitch marks (enough to lightly bond the layers together) or baste them together with needle and thread.
3. Stitch the border over the basting marks.
4. Stitch the shape for the aperture and stitch a second time, 2 to 3mm ($\frac{1}{12}$ to $\frac{1}{8}$in) away from the first line of stitching, to strengthen it.
5. Free-machine your design in the area between the aperture and the outer border, making sure that all the stitching links together and to the edge of the aperture and the border.
6. Stitch the design again, this time 2 to 3mm ($\frac{1}{12}$ to $\frac{1}{8}$in) away from the first line.
7. Place the mirror on the work to make sure that area of design is slightly larger than the mirror size. If it isn't, you will need to extend the design slightly.
8. Cut off any stray threads from the back of the work.
9. The next stage is to cut out selected areas. Do not cut out any areas within 1cm ($\frac{3}{8}$in) of the outer border, because the straight edge of the mirror will show if you do. Place the work on the glass and position the tip of the soldering iron right against the line of stitching. It will melt through all the layers to the glass. Move the tip slowly all around the stitching and the cut areas will pop out.
10. Score between the double line of stitching with the tip of the soldering iron to strengthen the design.
11. Create scrunchy textures in selected areas (see page 38).
12. Using the soldering iron, cut out the aperture as close as possible to the stitching. At this stage a piece of nylon organza can be bonded to the reverse side of the work if you wish.

Backing the mirror pocket
1. Place the work on the second piece of felt.
2. Machine around three sides only, stitching on the original border.
3. Slip the mirror inside the pocket, and slip the thin card behind it.

4. With the mirror in the pocket, carefully stitch the fourth side, feeling for the edge of the mirror as you stitch.
5. Stitch again around all four sides to strengthen the border.
6. To cut away the excess fabric, place the work on the glass and run the tip of the soldering iron as close as possible to the stitching, working all around the stitched border. You will be cutting through two pieces of felt, so move the tip slowly.

Below
The finished mirror. A cutwork design was stitched and selected areas were cut out.

CHAPTER THREE
THREE–DIMENSIONAL EFFECTS

Three-dimensional effects can be achieved by using products such as Wireform and metal grid. Wireform – a specialist metal mesh that is available in different weights and types of metal – can be sandwiched and stitched between fabrics, then manipulated into 3-D forms. Metal grid, the ordinary sort available from garden centres and DIY stores, can also be used as a framework for bonding and stitching fabrics.

Wireform between fabrics

For this sample, a design is scored around a metal template onto the layered strips of fabric. It is a good idea to practise drawing designs around the template on paper first (see page 44).

Requirements
- A strip of Wireform aluminium Studio Mesh, 1cm (³/₈in) diamond pattern – try not to bend the Wireform, and wear protective gloves when you cut it
- Old scissors to cut the Wireform
- Metal templates
- Machine needle size 100, sometimes known as a jeans needle
- Machine embroidery threads (non-meltable)
- Pins or needle and thread

For the top fabric:
- One piece of acrylic felt, 4 to 5cm (1½ to 2in) larger than the Wireform on all four sides.
- Four pieces of nylon organza, in a variety of colours, the same size as the felt, cut into strips of various widths and lengths
- A few narrow strips of iridescent synthetic fabric or other lightweight, contrasting synthetic fabric (non-stretch)

For the backing fabric:
- One piece of acrylic felt, the same size as the piece used for the top fabric

Method
1. Start by preparing the top fabric. Place the felt on the glass and then layer and overlap the strips evenly on the felt to a depth of at least three layers, adding some iridescent strips for contrast in the final layer.
2. Set the edge of the ruler on the edge of a strip and run the tip of the soldering iron down the ruler to lightly bond the strip down. Continue bonding all the edges of the strips. The aim is to bond all the strips together as invisibly as possible, until all the layers hold together in one piece.
3. Next, score the design. Note that the scored design should not reach to the very edges of the work as approximately 1cm (³/₈in) of waste fabric will be cut away on completion of the work. Holding a template firmly on the work, run the tip of the soldering iron around the template or part of the template. The tip will melt into the layers and score a mark at the same time as bonding the strips to the felt. Be careful not to score too heavily or you will cut through to the glass. Move the

Left
Wireform stitched between fabric. Some areas of the top layer have been removed, while others have been scored and marked.

template over the strips to create an interesting design all over them. See the diagram below for a suggestion.

4. Machine stitch a simple design that will integrate well with the scored design.
5. Place the Wireform on the backing felt and cover it with the prepared fabric.
6. Feel for the edge of the Wireform and pin or baste the top fabric to the backing felt, pinning at least 2cm (¾in) away from edge of the Wireform.
7. Stitch a border, following the line of pins or basting stitches. Remove the pins as you stitch or remove the basting stitches afterwards.
8. Place the work on the glass and, positioning the tip of the soldering iron at an upright angle against the edge of the stitching, slowly move it all around the border. This will bond the top fabric to the backing felt and cut off the excess fabric.
9. At this stage, more marks can be added to the design, but be careful not to score through to the Wireform.
10. Embellish the work with hand stitching.
11. Manipulate the finished piece into the required shape or form.

Further suggestion

- After step 7, the design could be machined through all the layers including the Wireform. When you machine stitch the Wireform between fabrics, the needle will hop to each side of the diamond mesh. However, it is advisable to use a strong needle, such as a jeans needle, which won't break if it hits the Wireform.

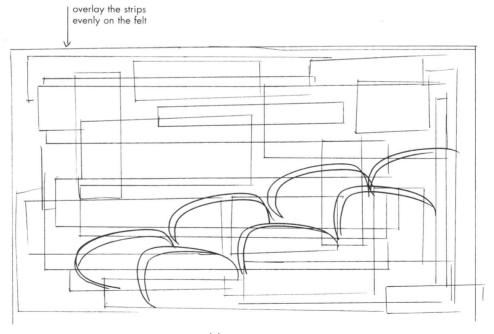

overlay the strips
evenly on the felt

score around the
template

Above
Wireform was stitched between felt and a top fabric made from strips bonded to acrylic felt. Marks were made on bonded strips.

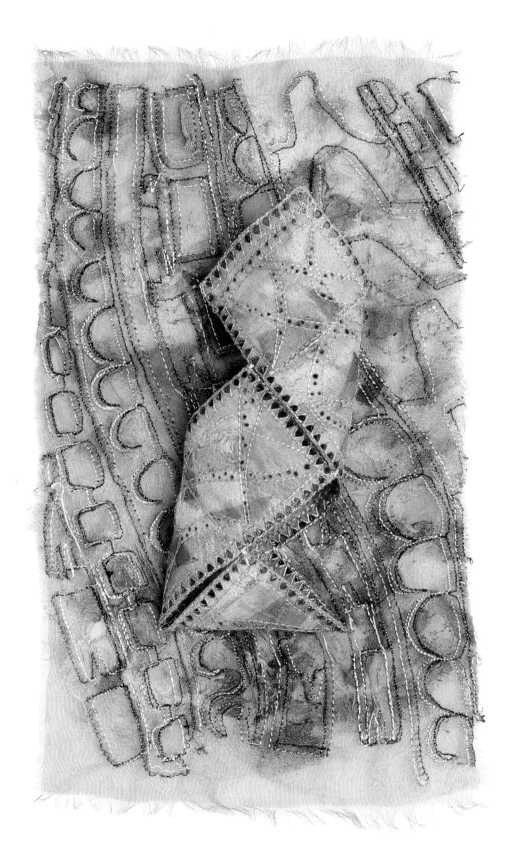

Right
Wireform Sparkle Mesh was stitched between a lightweight base fabric and a top fabric made of small pieces of nylon organza sandwiched between two larger pieces of nylon organza. The work was finished with a lacy border.

Lacy borders

Wireform Sparkle Mesh is a very lightweight aluminium mesh with a fine diamond pattern. It lends itself to creating more delicate pieces of work, and can be used without a felt backing. Here, Sparkle Mesh has been stitched between two lightweight synthetic fabrics and finished with a lacy border. See also page 127.

Method
1. Take a strip of Wireform Sparkle Mesh, place it between two pieces of lightweight synthetic fabric and stitch with a simple design.
2. Stitch a border 2mm (¹⁄₁₂in) away from the outer edge of the Wireform, using a running stitch.
3. Change to zigzag stitch, and stitch a line of zigzag on the outside edge of the border, so that the zigzag just touches the stitched line.
4. Change back to running stitch. Stitch around the outside edge of the zigzag so that the stitching just touches the edge of the zigzag.
5. Placing the work on the glass, position the tip of the soldering iron on the edge of the outer line of running stitches and move it slowly around the stitching. This will seal the edges and cut off the excess fabric.
6. Hold the work and push the tip of the soldering iron through the triangular shapes of the zigzag stitching. Push the tip through as far as it will go and move it around until it has melted away all the fabric, leaving only the lacy zigzag thread (see diagram below). The stitching will be stiffened with the melted fabric.

Further suggestions
• Experiment with altering the width and length of the zigzag stitch.
• To make a lacy fabric, stitch row after row of automatic stitch patterns and then melt away the fabric between the patterns with the tip of the soldering iron.

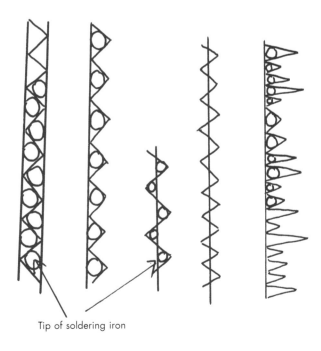

Tip of soldering iron

Metal grid

For more robust work you need very strong metal grid, which is sold in DIY stores. The squares of the grid are 1.5cm (⅝in) each way. Wear protective gloves and use wire cutters to cut the grid. You will be stitching over the bars of the grid, and you might find that it takes a little practice to get into the rhythm of the stitching and avoid hitting the metal bars with the needle.

For this sample, you will require a piece of metal grid, which you could spray with quick-drying metallic spray paint first. This is best done on a protected surface outdoors, to lessen the risk of breathing in any fumes.

Method

1. First assemble a piece of metal grid, a piece of acrylic felt that is larger than the grid, two pieces of organza the same size as the felt and snippets of nylon organza. Layer them in this order: acrylic felt at the bottom, a piece of nylon organza, the snippets, the metal grid and then the second piece of nylon organza.
2. Pin all around the outer border of the grid to secure it between the top and bottom pieces of fabric.
3. Stitch all around the border, stitching as close as possible to the edge of the grid and removing the pins as you stitch. Change to zigzag stitch, with the width setting slightly wider than the width of the metal bars.
4. Starting at the centre top of the grid, manually move the control wheel to check that the needle is not going to hit the metal bar. Slowly zigzag over the bars, lifting the foot if necessary to hop over the cross sections (diagram A below shows result).
5. By hand or machine, stitch simple patterns in the squares of the grid (see diagram B below).
6. Place the work on the glass and make marks between the stitched patterns with the tip of the soldering iron.
7. Run the tip of the soldering iron around the border to seal the layers and cut off the excess fabric.
8. Bend the grid into an undulating form.

A

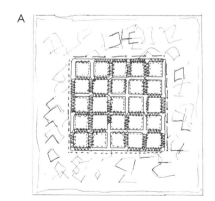

B

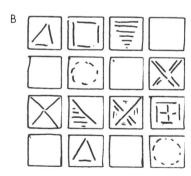

Above
A metal grid was machine-stitched between layers of acrylic felt and synthetic fabrics. Marks were made with the soldering iron and the work was manipulated into an undulating form.

Three-dimensional effects 95

Above
Metal grid was stitched between silk and polyester organzas. Using the reverse appliqué method, some areas of the top layer were cut back to reveal the colours below while others were cut back as far as the silk underneath. The piece was rolled and laced through eyelets, which were made with the tip of the soldering iron.

Above
Metal grid hand-stitched between fabric, with cross stitch at the intersections and lazy daisy and straight stitch in the squares, finished with mark-making.

Weaving through a metal grid

Here, strips have been woven through a metal grid. For further embellishment, you could spray the grid with metallic paint. Note that the length of the strips should be longer than the grid to allow for the amount of fabric taken up when weaving them through the bars.

Method

1. First assemble your fabrics: two pieces of acrylic felt, one piece of nylon organza the same size as the felt, snippets of nylon organza in various colours, plus one piece of synthetic fabric slightly heavier than the nylon organza.
2. Place one piece of felt on the glass and cover it with a layer of the organza snippets.
3. Cover the snippets with the square of nylon organza.
4. Cut the layered fabrics into strips with the soldering iron along the edge of a metal ruler, cutting the strips slightly narrower than the width between the bars of the grid. The number of strips cut should equal the number of horizontal bars in the grid.
5. Put these weft strips to one side.
6. To prepare the strips for the padding, cover the second piece of felt with the synthetic fabric and cut into strips as before.
7. Place a padding strip so that it sits between the first two vertical bars down the right-hand side of the grid.
8. Take a weft strip and start weaving across the top row of squares, from right to left. Weave under the first bar, over the padding strip, then under the second bar. Place the next padding strip in position between the vertical bars and weave over it. Weave all along the top row of bars until all the padding strips are held in place.
9. Weave the rest of the strips over the padding strips down the length of the grid.
10. Marks can be made on the strips at this stage, either freehand or through a metal stencil.
11. Manipulate the work into shape.

Right and far right
Fabric was stitched with a series of parallel horizontal lines and then cut into strips with a soldering iron. Each strip was machine-stitched with a few decorative lines before being woven through a metal grid. The marks were scored through a metal alphabet template.

CHAPTER FOUR
OTHER MATERIALS

This chapter gives ideas for using additional materials to add texture and interest to your work. It begins with a few quick and easy methods of adding colour to acrylic felt, then goes on to discuss methods for working with specialist materials such as Bondaweb, which can be ironed onto acrylic felt to give an interesting surface; stencil film, which can be bonded to fabric as well as used for cutting out stencils; foils, which add an instant metallic touch to your work; and natural fabrics.

Paints

ACRYLIC PAINT

Acrylic paint works very well on acrylic felt and can produce strong colours, depending on the extent to which the paints are diluted with water. I have used the standard size of acrylic felt for all of the painting techniques. Below are three easy methods for colouring acrylic felt with acrylic paint. I suggest you prepare several sample pieces to use later.
- Lightly dampen the surface of the felt with a sponge and apply diluted acrylic paint with a sponge or brush.
- Print patterns or motifs using wooden blocks.
- Brush or sponge paint through stencils.

WATER-SOLUBLE PAINTS

Brusho, which is the type I use, is available in powder or solid form. It is a non-permanent paint, used for design work, but I like the effect it gives on acrylic felt when coated with Bondaweb. Wear rubber gloves to protect your hands from staining. Below are three methods for using Brusho, or similar paints, on felt.
- Simply paint the block form onto damp felt with a brush.
- Mix the powder form with water and then paint or sponge it onto the felt.
- Sprinkle the dry powder lightly onto damp felt, using more than one colour. The colours are very strong and blend together beautifully. Do not make the felt very wet and be careful, as a little Brusho goes a long way.

Bondaweb (fusible webbing)

Bondaweb is an adhesive webbing, backed with silicon paper. The surface texture feels rough or gritty due to the adhesive, which melts when heated. It is designed to bond fabrics such as curtain hems, but for several years embroiderers have been using it far more creatively. Ironing Bondaweb onto acrylic felt gives a soft, smooth, leathery surface.

PAINTING BONDAWEB

Painted Bondaweb can be ironed to all sorts of fabric to add interest, colour and texture. Below are three easy methods for colouring Bondaweb.
- Carefully paint or sponge the rough-textured surface of the Bondaweb with acrylic paint or Brusho, blending the colours, and leave to dry naturally. When the paint dries, the Bondaweb will have a wrinkly, wavy surface.
- Paint or sponge two or three colours of metallic acrylic paint onto Bondaweb.
- Paint or sponge a mixture of metallic and plain colours onto Bondaweb.

Left
This piece was created using foil fabric and Wireform, with nylon organza.

IRONING BONDAWEB TO ACRYLIC FELT

When painted Bondaweb is ironed onto a piece of acrylic felt, baking parchment is used to protect the iron, which should not be in steam mode.

Method
1. Place the Bondaweb on the felt, painted side down, and cover the silicon backing paper with the baking parchment.
2. Iron over the baking parchment with a medium-to-hot iron.
3. Wait for the silicon paper to cool, then peel it off carefully. The surface of the Bondaweb will only become sticky again if it is reheated.

Further suggestion
• Iron painted Bondaweb to handmade textured paper, or to paper in a sketchbook, and draw on it using a permanent marker.

PAINTED ACRYLIC FELT AND BONDAWEB

Both the acrylic felt and the Bondaweb can be painted before they are bonded together, the latter with metallic acrylic paints. Again, baking parchment is used to protect the iron, which should not be in steam mode.

Method
1. Place the Bondaweb, painted side down, on the painted felt and cover the silicon paper with the baking parchment.
2. Iron over the baking parchment to bond the painted Bondaweb onto the painted felt.
3. Wait for the silicon paper to cool and then carefully peel it off.

SANDWICH SAMPLE

For extra detail, snippets of lightweight synthetic fabrics can be sandwiched between painted acrylic felt and Bondaweb painted with metallic acrylic paint. You could use snippets from a range of lightweight fabrics such as organza, net or lamé.

Method
1. Scatter snippets of synthetic fabric over the painted felt.
2. Place the Bondaweb, painted side down, on the snippets and cover the silicon paper with baking parchment.
3. Iron over the baking parchment with a medium-to-hot iron (no steam).
4. Wait for the silicon paper to cool and then carefully peel it off.

Further suggestions
• Iron plain Bondaweb to plain felt and draw a design on the smooth surface with a permanent marker.

Above
Snippets of fabric were layered onto felt and painted, then Bondaweb was ironed over them. The shapes were cut out around a metal template, repositioned and marked. The piece was then stitched to a background of painted Bondaweb on felt.

Stencil film

Transparent stencil film is used for cutting out stencils, but I also combine it with fabric and Bondaweb. The film is usually sold in A4 size. Stencil designs may be cut as described below.

Cutting out stencils

Method
1. Draw or trace the design onto the stencil film, using a fine-tipped permanent marker.
2. Place the stencil film on the glass.
3. Cut the design out of the film with the tip of the soldering iron. Alternatively, draw your design on paper and place it underneath the glass, then put the stencil film on the glass and cut out the design.

Further suggestions
• Use metal templates to cut out shapes to make up the stencil design.

Left
Shapes were drawn onto the stencil film with a permanent marker then cut out with the soldering iron. They were then stencilled onto felt with black acrylic paint.

Far left
Painted Bondaweb was ironed over snippets of fabric on felt, covered with stencil film and stitched. Some negative areas were cut out; others were scored heavily with the soldering iron to create a textured surface.

Bonding stencil film to synthetic fabric

Stencil film may be bonded to synthetic fabrics such as lightweight polyester, lamé, lace and net. Here, a coin is used as a template for the design – do take care, as coins can get a little hot.

Method
1. Place the stencil film on the glass and cover it with a piece of lightweight synthetic fabric, such as polyester lamé.
2. Cover the fabric with a lightweight synthetic lace, preferably one with an interesting design on it.
3. Place a coin on the work and run the tip of the soldering iron all around the edge of the coin at an upright angle. All layers will bond together and the cut shape will easily pop out.

Further suggestions
- Change the order in which the fabric and film are layered.
- Sandwiching fabrics and acrylic felt between two pieces of stencil film produces a rigid fabric, very suitable for jewellery, book covers or boxes.

Left and right
Buttons combining lace, foil, organza, printed fabrics, stencil film and acrylic felt, stitched to a backing of organza shapes bonded to acrylic felt.

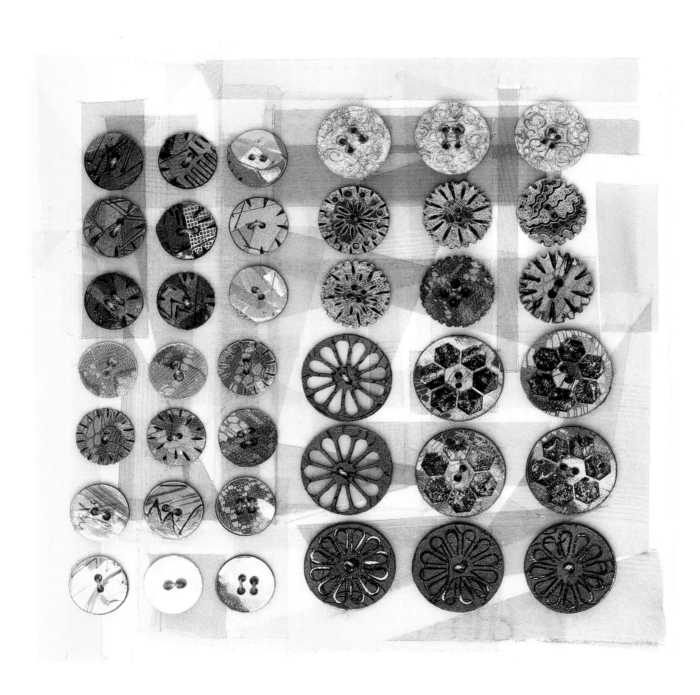

Four-sided straws

These straws are made from stencil film and have approximately 1cm ($^3/_8$in) sides. Start with a piece of film 10cm (4in) square until you have made a few, then try using a larger piece to make longer, wider straws.

Method

1. Place a piece of film on the glass. Take the bottom edge of the film and carefully bend it, without creasing, 2.5cm (1in) up from the bottom. Tilt and press the edge of the ruler firmly on the film, 5mm ($^1/_4$in) down from the edge. Run the tip of the soldering iron slowly along the edge of the ruler to seal the two layers together. Keep the ruler in position and remove the excess film.
2. Now run the soldering iron along the edge of the ruler again to reinforce the seal. You should now have a hollow tube, with the seam at the top.
3. Carefully squash the tube so that the seam is centre front.
4. Squash the tube flat by running it between your thumb and fingers to make a firm crease along top and bottom edges.
5. Squash the tube again so that the seam is now at the bottom and make a firm crease along the top edge.
6. Carefully press on the sides to allow the film to pop into a four-sided straw shape.

Further suggestions for straws

*   Cover the film with a synthetic sheer fabric and then continue as above. The fabric can be on the inside or outside of the straw.
*   Make a design of marks and patterns or holes on the sides of the straws with the soldering iron.
*   Make longer, fatter straws.
*   Make tiny straws resembling bugle beads.
*   Bond fragments of fabric to the film before folding and sealing it.

Further suggestions for stencil film

*   Try using acetate film with a design photocopied onto it.
*   Iron painted Bondaweb onto stencil film or acrylic felt. The stencil film is quite thick and will stand a fairly hot iron, but if you prefer you could cover it with a sheet of baking parchment to protect the iron.
*   Iron painted Bondaweb onto acrylic felt and cover it with stencil film. Cover with baking parchment and iron the film to the felt. Wait for the film to cool down and then carefully peel it off the felt. A thin layer of the film will remain on the felt, giving it a very shiny surface. Try using this technique on synthetic velvet.
*   Some films buckle or distort with the heat of the iron, but this too can produce some interesting results.
*   Use a hot air tool to distort the stencil film.

Above
Four-sided straws made using a variety
of fabrics bonded to stencil film.

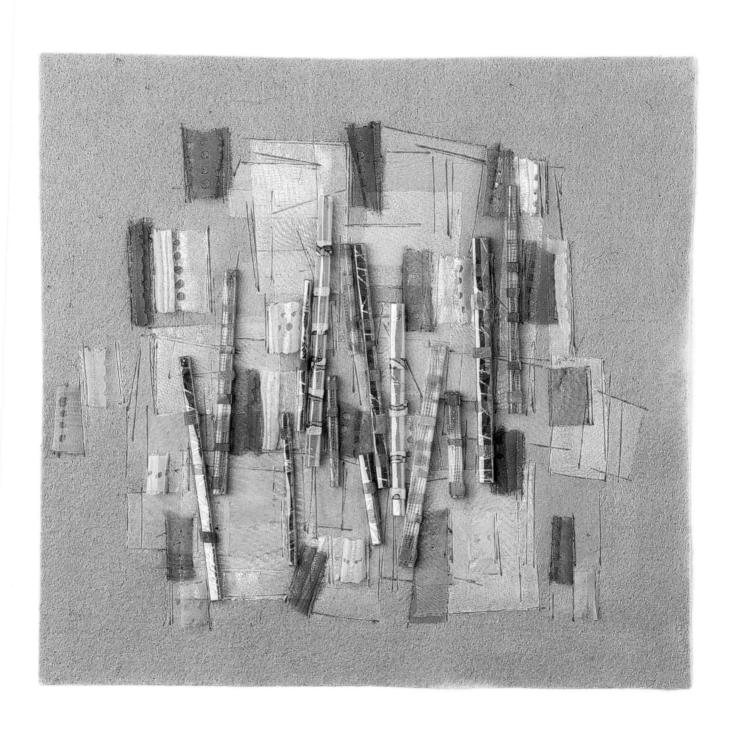

Above
These stencil film straws feature a variety
of fabrics bonded to stencil film.

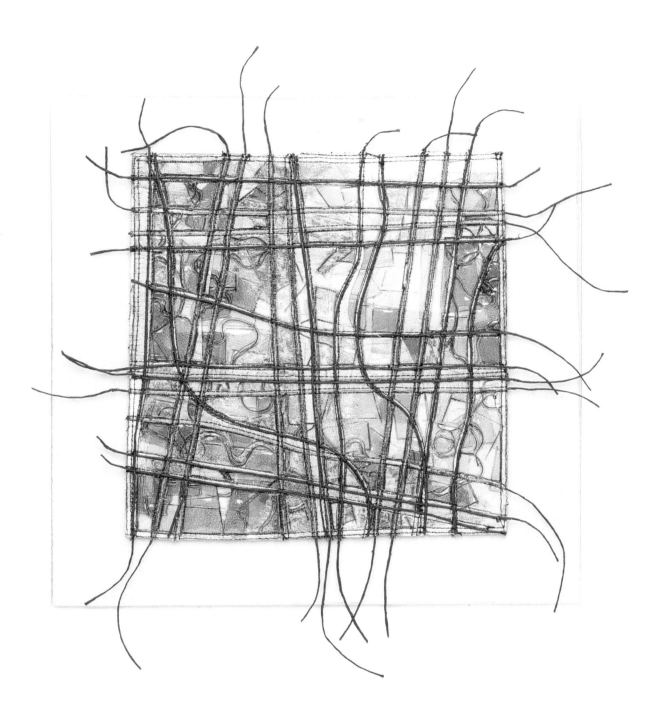

Above

A mosaic of nylon organza was layered over acrylic felt and covered with a piece of clear plastic film. Lengths of paper string were stretched taut across the film and pinned firmly at the ends. The work was then covered with a piece of nylon organza. A twin needle was used to stitch over the lengths of string. Some areas of the top layer of organza were then removed using the reverse appliqué technique. Other areas of the surface of the plastic were stippled with the tip of the soldering iron to create a textured frosty and opaque effect. Finally, some lengths of paper string were hand-couched over the work.

Foils

All sorts of different foils can be used with the techniques in this book, both ones specially produced for the purpose and ordinary foils used for packaging. Some will bond without using an adhesive, others won't – it is usually a matter of experimentation.

Transfoil

Transfoil is a very thin, film-like plastic version of gold leaf, with a clear protective covering. It is usually bonded to surfaces with an adhesive. This sample was made with a combination of acrylic felt painted with acrylic paint, Bondaweb lightly painted with gold acrylic paint and Transfoil.

Method

1. Protecting the iron with baking parchment, iron the painted Bondaweb onto the painted acrylic felt.
2. Place a piece of Transfoil on the glass and use the soldering iron to cut shapes, either freehand or around a template.
3. Place the Transfoil shapes, shiny side up, on the painted Bondaweb.
4. Cover with a sheet of baking parchment.
5. Iron over the baking parchment to bond the Transfoil to the painted Bondaweb.
6. Carefully remove the baking parchment when it has cooled down.
7. Peel the protective clear covering off the foil.

Below
Transfoil shapes were cut with the soldering iron, then ironed onto acrylic felt coated with painted Bondaweb.

Above

A foil-coated fabric was painted with acrylic paints, placed on a base of acrylic felt and then cut and bonded into three pieces with the soldering iron. Painted Bondaweb was ironed to the largest piece to use for the base. The second piece was covered with snippets of Transfoil and painted Bondaweb was ironed on top. The smallest piece had a few snippets of Transfoil bonded to it. Finally narrow strips of painted foil-coated fabric were bonded across the centre.

Foil packaging

Many types of foil packaging can be cut, bonded and marked with the soldering iron. Look for the heavyweight packets used for coffee, rice, dried fruit and crisps. These are often in jewel-like colours and the reverse side is usually silver. Experiment with packaging using some of the cutting, bonding and mark-making techniques described earlier in the book. Try the following:

1. Cut strips of foil packaging and bond them together using the patchwork technique.
2. Place the strips onto acrylic felt, then cut out shapes, either freehand or around a template.

Further suggestions

*   Some fashion fabrics are coated with foil and have a smooth, shiny surface. These fabrics bond very well to other synthetic fabrics and the shiny surface can be painted, printed on or drawn on with permanent markers.
*   Fishing tackle shops often sell a wide range of interesting foils.

Right
Motifs bonded between stencil film on a background of PVC.

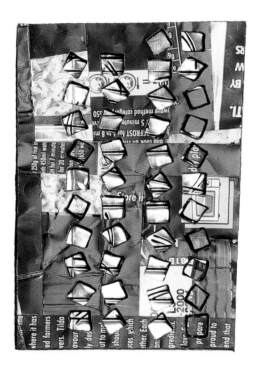

Above
Strips of foil packaging and fabric bonded together, plus foil packaging on acrylic felt with shapes cut out around a template.

Left

Foil-coated fabric on a base of acrylic felt was painted with acrylic paints and covered with nylon organza. Spirals were stitched and then cut with the soldering iron and stretched. Finally the work was stitched to a background made of bonded waste nylon organza scraps.

Above

A strip of fabric made up of waste nylon organza (see page 41) was placed on acrylic felt and covered with a piece of blue foil-coated fabric. A metal template was placed on the foil and scored around with the tip of the soldering iron. The excess foil was then carefully removed. The negative shapes in the foil were bonded to a mosaic of organza, backed with acrylic felt.

PVC fabric

PVC fabric is widely used in the fashion industry and is available in a variety of metallic colours, including gold and silver. You can cut, bond and make marks on PVC: I like to use it supported by acrylic felt or a similar non-stretchy fabric.

Above

ALHAMBRA PALACE

Square nylon organza shapes were bonded to gold PVC to form a tile pattern. Shadowy images of people were cut freehand and bonded lightly to the tile shapes. The intricate cutwork design in the foreground was traced onto polyester organza, which was tacked to acrylic felt and then stitched. The cutwork was done from the front of the work and stitched to the PVC background.

Right

Using differently shaped templates and a variety of fabrics, shapes were bonded to PVC on acrylic felt. The tip of the soldering iron was scored around a metal template to bond the fabric to the PVC and felt. With a careful tearing action, the excess fabric was removed from around the template. It takes a little practice as the depth of the scored line varies with different types of fabric.

Project: Brooches

These brooch designs offer a way of using a range of cut shapes and sizes, such as small squares, triangles and circles, made in previous techniques. In addition to the PVC, or similar fabric, you will need stencil film, two pieces of acrylic felt and a piece of synthetic lace or net. It will be helpful to refer to the instructions for mark-making and bonding on shapes in chapter 1 (20 and 67). The designs shown here were made with a metal ruler about 6cm (2½in) wide.

Method

1. To prepare square bases for the brooches, first place one piece of felt on the glass and cover it with the PVC.
2. Place the ruler 1cm (⅜in) down from the top edge and run the tip of the soldering iron along the edge to bond the two fabrics together and to cut off the excess.
3. Moving the ruler down the fabric, cut a number of strips the width of the ruler, and then cut the strips into squares.
4. Make marks on the squares (see page 20).
5. Taking another piece of felt and more PVC, now place lace or net on top of the PVC, and repeat steps 1 to 4, cutting a range of sizes.
6. Bond the small shapes to the square PVC bases (see page 67).

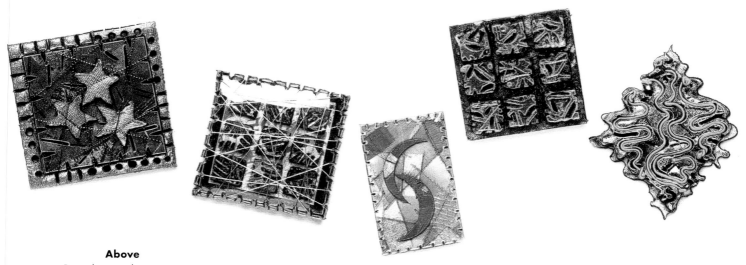

Above
Brooches made from foil, stencil film, glitzy fabrics such as Angelina, and polyester organza on an acrylic felt base.

7. Place one brooch on a second piece of felt and cover it with stencil film. The film and felt must be at least 3cm (1¼in) larger than the brooch on all four sides.
8. To bond the stencil film over the brooch, tilt and press the edge of the metal ruler very firmly on the film at the very edge of the PVC square.
9. Rest the tip of the soldering iron on the edge of the ruler, 2cm (¾in) to the left of the square. Run the tip along the ruler beyond the end of the square by 2cm (¾in), making sure the tip is in good contact with the side of the square in order to melt and bond all the layers together.
10. Repeat on the opposite side and then the remaining two sides.
11. Press the tip of the soldering iron sideways into each of the sides of the brooch to make notches.
12. Wrap threads around the brooch through the notches, and finish off with a stitch on the reverse side.

Above

TREAD SOFTLY

The design was based on the patterns on a tower of old car tyres. It was traced onto cold-water-soluble fabric. Snippets of nylon organza were layered over silk organza and then covered with the soluble fabric and basted. The design was free-machined and the soluble fabric was washed away. The work was ironed while wet to press and dry it. The snippets of nylon organza were then blended together with the tip of the soldering iron. Large areas of the silk organza backing fabric were left unstitched and were cut out using very fine sharp embroidery scissors. The finished piece falls into soft folds.

Combining natural and synthetic fabrics

There is a certain amount of adherence when bonding a natural fabric to a synthetic fabric. It is by no means as permanent as bonding synthetic fabrics to each other, but it is very useful as a temporary bond before stitching. You might like to try some of the following suggestions.

- Overlap strips of natural and synthetic fabrics and bond them to a synthetic fabric.
- Bond synthetic fabric to cotton velvet.
- Bond through loosely woven linen scrim onto synthetic fabric.
- Bond synthetic fabric to handmade paper.
- Layer synthetic fragments with natural fabrics. Stitch them together and blend the fabrics together with the tip of the soldering iron; the natural fabrics will bond a little with the synthetic types.

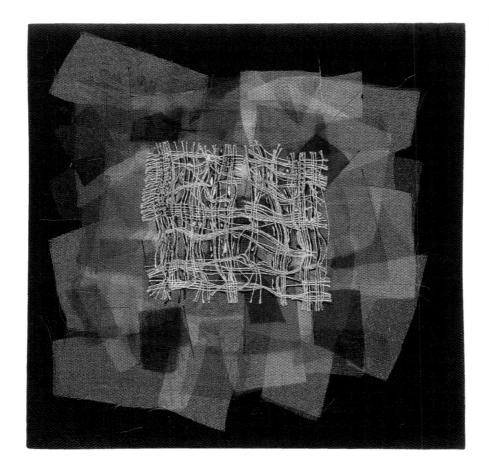

Left
Nylon organza was bonded to acrylic felt and a piece of linen scrim was placed on top. The scrim was covered with a nylon net. Marks were scored through the net along the warp and weft of the linen.

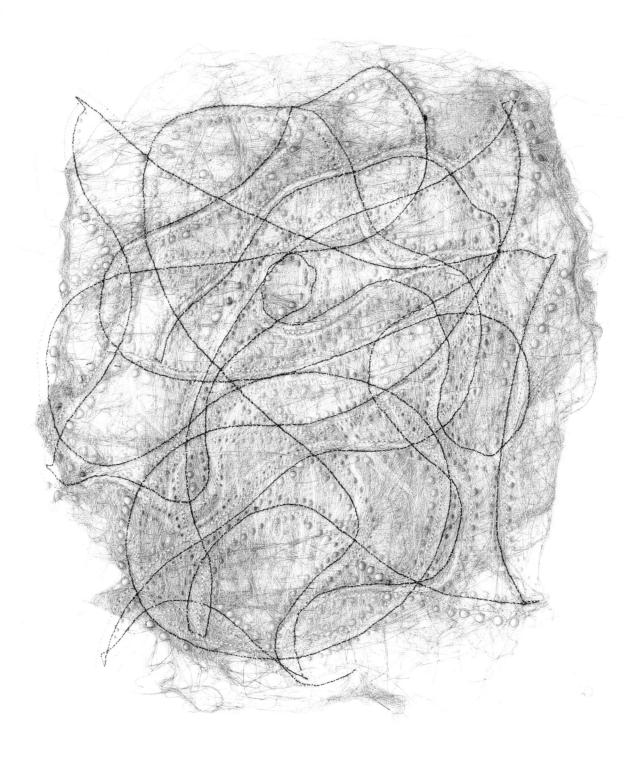

Above
Hand-made linen was twin-needled to white acrylic felt. The tip of the soldering iron was pushed though to make the eyelets.

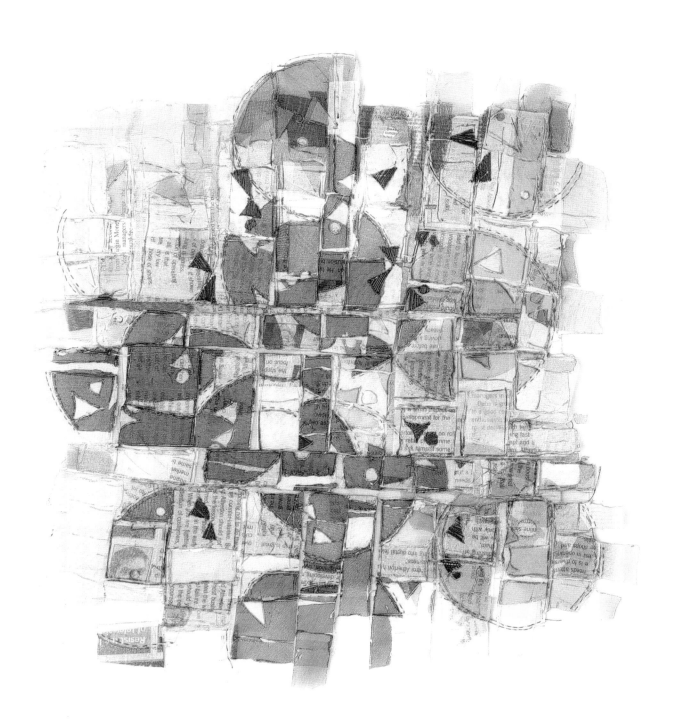

Above
Newspaper, interleaved with polyester organza, bonded to a base of acrylic felt with the soldering iron and then cut into strips. The strips were woven and the design was stitched over them. Marks were scored and some layers were cut back.

Suppliers

UK
Art Van Go
The Studios
1 Stevenage Road
Knebworth
Hertfordshire SG3 6AN
Tel: 01438 814 946
www.artvango.co.uk
Face masks, fine-tipped soldering irons, heat tools, materials for printing and painting on fabric, respirators, Transfoil and Wireform.

Margaret Beal Embroidery
01264 365102
Email: burning.issues@margaretbeal.co.uk
Fine-tipped soldering irons, stencil film, acrylic felt and organzas, foil fabric and PVC.

Gill Sew
Boundary Lane
Moor Common
Lane End
Buckinghamshire HP14 3HR
Email: gillsew@ukonline.co.uk
Printing blocks and machine embroidery threads

Inca Studio
10 Duke Street
Princes Risborough
Buckinghamshire HP27 0AT
Tel: 01844 343 343
Email: studioinca@aol.com
www.incastudio.com
Machine embroidery threads

Mulberry Silks
Silkwood
4 Park Close
Tetbury
Gloucestershire GL8 8HS
Email: patricia.wood@rdplus.net
www.mulberrysilks-patriciawood.com
Silk threads, silk organza, ribbons

USA
MeinkeToy
PMB 411
55 E Long Lake Road
Troy, MI 48085
USA
tel: 248 813 9866
www.meinketoy.com
email: meinketoy@mindspring.com
General craft supplies

AUSTRALIA
The Thread Studio
6 Smith Street
Perth 6000
Western Australia
Tel: +61 (0)9 227 1561
Email: dale@thethreadstudio.com
www.thethreadstudio.com
Soldering irons and most supplies

NEW ZEALAND
Craft Supplies
31 Gurney Road
Belmont
Lower Hut
New Zealand
Tel: 044 565 00544
General craft supplies

Further reading

Beaney, Jan and Littlejohn, Jean. *Bonding and Beyond*. Double Trouble Enterprises, 1999
Beaney, Jan and Littlejohn, Jean. *Transfer to Transform*. Double Trouble Enterprises, 1999
Campbell-Harding, Valerie and Watts, Pamela. *Machine Embroidery Stitch Techniques*.
    B T Batsford, 2004
Hedley, Gwen. *Surfaces for Stitch*. B T Batsford, 2000
Issett, Ruth. *Colour on Paper and Fabric*. Batsford, 1998
Talbot, Margaret. *Medieval Flushwork of East Anglia*. Poppyland Publishing, 2004
    (for perfect images to use for design and mark-making ideas). Tel: 01359 240693
Watts, Pamela. *Beginners Guide to Machine Embroidery*. Search Press, 2003

Workshop on the Web: www.workshopontheweb.com

Below
3-D forms made from
Wireform Sparkle
Mesh finished with
lacy borders.

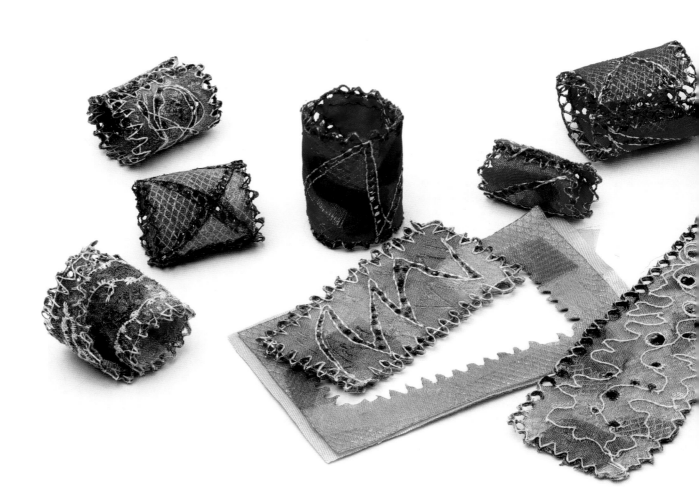

Index